hamlyn | all colour cookbook

KU-500-244

200 wok recipes

Marina Filippelli

An Hachette UK company
www.hachette.co.uk

First published in Great Britain in 2009 by Hamlyn,
a division of Octopus Publishing Group Ltd
2–4 Heron Quays, London E14 4JP
www.octopusbooks.co.uk

Copyright © Octopus Publishing Group Ltd 2009

Some of the recipes in this book have previously appeared
in other books published by Hamlyn.

ISBN: 978-0-600-61862-1

A CIP catalogue record for this book is available from the
British Library.

Printed and bound in China

2 3 4 5 6 7 8 9 10

Both metric and imperial measurements have been given
in all recipes. Use one set of measurements only, and not
a mixture of both.

Standard level spoon measurements are used in all recipes.
1 tablespoon = one 15 ml spoon
1 teaspoon = one 5 ml spoon.

Fresh herbs should be used unless otherwise stated.

Medium eggs should be used unless otherwise stated.

The Department of Health advises that eggs should not be
consumed raw. This book contains some dishes made with
raw or lightly cooked eggs. It is prudent for vulnerable
people such as pregnant and nursing mothers, invalids, the
elderly, babies and young children to avoid uncooked or
lightly cooked dishes made with eggs. Once prepared, these
dishes should be kept refrigerated and used promptly.

This book includes dishes made with nuts and nut
derivatives. It is advisable for those with known allergic
reactions to nuts and nut derivatives and those who may be
potentially vulnerable to these allergies, such as pregnant and
nursing mothers, invalids, the elderly, babies and children, to
avoid dishes made with nuts and nut oils. It is also prudent to
check the labels of pre-prepared ingredients for the possible
inclusion of nut derivatives.

200 wok recipes

contents

introduction

introduction

Versatile and efficient, the wok was invented by the Chinese but was soon adopted by cooks throughout east and southeast Asia. With its ability to sear food quickly, it's the perfect pan for stir-frying, the large, sloped sides giving plenty of space to toss the ingredients around for quick, even cooking.

The technique looks deceptively simple – anyone who has tried cooking with a wok knows it can so easily go wrong. But if you master the basic rules of stir-frying described below, your wok will become your best friend in the kitchen. Useful for both quick weekday meals and for stress-free entertaining, a wok is also handy for more than stir-frying. Those in the know use their woks for steaming, braising, deep-frying and smoking.

cooking techniques

It's easy when you know how. The following tips will help you make the most of your wok.

stir-frying

Speed is of the essence. Cut all ingredients into small pieces that will cook quickly. Meat or fish should cook in a maximum of 4–5 minutes, while vegetables need to be cut to ensure even cooking – no big broccoli florets next to finely sliced carrots. Add tender vegetables such as bean sprouts at the end of cooking so that they keep their crispness.

Any weighing, slicing or chopping needs to be done before you start cooking. Remember, you're cooking on fierce heat, so if you start preparing the vegetables once the garlic and ginger are already in the pan, you'll end up with a burnt mess. Keep all your prepared ingredients to hand in separate bowls, ready to be tipped into the wok at the right moment.

Choose the right cuts. Because stir-frying is such a fast method of cooking, it's suited only to lean cuts of meat that don't need extended cooking to become tender. Fillet or sirloin, trimmed of fat, are the perfect beef cuts. Use fillet or loin when cooking with pork

or lamb, and breast when cooking with chicken or duck. Seafood such as prawns, scallops and squid are fantastic for stir-frying: they cook in minutes and have a firm texture that doesn't break up with the constant stirring. Delicate fish that flake easily once cooked should be rejected in favour of firm fish such as monkfish.

Get the wok smoking hot before you start. Place the wok over a high heat, add the suggested amount of oil and then let it get nice and hot. This will take a while, as the heat needs to travel from the narrow base all the way to the wide brim. Swirl the oil around so that it coats the sides of the wok as well as the base. You want it to get seriously hot before adding any ingredients so that they'll sear and brown quickly as you toss them around the pan. Look out for the oil starting to shimmer in the pan: this is the sign that you can start cooking.

Stir-fry in small batches. As soon as you add ingredients to the wok, the temperature drops dramatically. Since the aim is to sear the meat or fish in fierce heat, try to avoid overcrowding the wok. Brown the meat or fish first (in batches, if necessary), then remove it from the pan, stir-fry the vegetables and return the meat at the end. If you cook everything in one go, the meat or fish will stew in the vegetable juices rather than brown.

Keep stirring. Constantly moving the food around ensures even cooking and prevents ingredients from burning over the high heat.

Add liquid to finish the cooking. Once the ingredients have been seared and browned, act quickly to avoid them scorching in the high heat. This is when you can add some liquid to the pan, sending a gust of steam through the wok to finish off the cooking. A dash of water or stock does the trick, but you could also inject an extra level of flavour into the stir-fry with ingredients such as Chinese rice wine, soy sauce or oyster sauce.

steaming and smoking

A large wok with a domed lid is perfect for steaming or smoking. For steaming, simply place the food directly on a perforated stand in a wok half-filled with steaming water, cover with a lid and leave the food to cook in the trapped steam. The same principles apply to smoking, but instead of using water to create steam, the smoked recipes in this book use tea leaves that burn on the base of the lidded wok to create smoke.

A larger than usual wok is best for steaming or smoking because it provides ample room for the steam or smoke to circulate, so cooking the food evenly. The wide diameter also makes it easy to get the food in and out without burning yourself.

Many wok sets come with wire racks to support the food, but you could also use a number of implements to do the same job, such as a bamboo steamer, a foldable steaming rack or a metal trivet, or simply stand a plate of food on upturned ramekins. In fact, anything that will remain firmly in place and support the dish with the food to be steamed will do.

deep-frying

Its wide diameter also makes your wok ideal for deep-frying. Food has plenty of space to circulate in the oil and crisp up evenly, and adding and removing the food is easier than in pans with a narrower circumference.

braising and stewing

Just like any other large pan with a lid, the wok can also be used for braising or stewing. There are no particular benefits to using a wok rather than a saucepan for this purpose, but this extra versatility makes the wok even more useful in the kitchen.

healthy cooking

It's a myth that all stir-fries are healthy. Overdo it with the sauces or get your stir-frying technique wrong and you could miss out on the healthy benefits of a stir-fry. Done properly, the technique requires only a small amount of oil and, because of the speed of cooking, results in a minimal loss of nutrients. Furthermore, it's a method of cooking that uses lean cuts of meat and is also a great way for the whole family to get their daily dose of vegetables.

Use your wok for steaming, and you're choosing what is probably the healthiest cooking technique of all. One of the great advantages of steaming is that the flavour and goodness of the food is preserved. The food cooks in the vapour created by the steaming liquid rather than in the cooking liquid itself, so there is less loss of water-soluble vitamins than occurs with boiling or poaching. There's also the additional advantage that you don't need to use any oil or fat when steaming.

choosing a wok

The traditional round-based woks are perfect for using on a gas hob, while the modern flat-based woks were specifically developed to be used on electric hobs. Woks come either with two side handles or with one long handle. The latter is ideal for stir-frying, as you can hold the wok steady with one hand and use your spare hand for the vigorous stirring. A long handle also enables you to keep the wok balanced while still standing at a distance from any oil splashes. The two-handled wok is probably best for steaming or deep-frying, giving you more control when you need to move it full of liquid.

There are many nonstick woks available now, some of which look gorgeous, and these are fantastic if you want to cut down on the quantity of oil you need for stir-frying. However, there is absolutely no need to spend a lot of money on a wok: the traditional carbon steel woks available from Chinese or Asian stores cost next to nothing and can last you a lifetime if cared for properly.

Whichever style of wok you buy, make sure it's a large one. A successful stir-fry depends on high heat with plenty of space for the food to be tossed around. Squash the food in a

small space, and it will just steam and sweat. Go for a wok that is at least 30 cm (12 inches) in diameter.

caring for your wok

Unless you buy a nonstick version, your wok will need to be proved, or 'seasoned', before using. Wash your new purchase thoroughly in soapy water to remove any greasy coating it might have been given by the manufacturer. Dry it thoroughly, then place it on a hob over a low heat. Rub it all over with a piece of kitchen paper dipped in vegetable oil and leave it heating for 10 minutes. Wipe off the oil with more kitchen paper, then repeat the process until the paper doesn't blacken when you wipe off the oil. A well-seasoned wok will stir-fry beautifully!

After each use, wash the wok with water, using a plastic brush but never a wire scrub. It then needs to be dried thoroughly to avoid any rust, so put it over a low heat until any moisture steams dry. A quick wipe with kitchen paper dipped in vegetable oil will give your wok further protection against rust.

If you plan on steaming a lot, you might be better off buying two woks. Boiling water ruins the seal that the proving gives to the surface of the wok, so the seasoning process described above has to be repeated before stir-frying again. This is no big deal, but it would be a little laborious if your plan is to steam and stir-fry regularly!

extra equipment

If you're a dab hand at using chopsticks, you might want to pick up long wooden chopsticks next time you visit a Chinese store. They're great for stirring food around the wok and make lifting large pieces of deep-fried food out of the oil very easy.

Spatulas or wooden spoons are both perfect for use in stir-frying.

A domed wok lid is essential if you are planning to do more than just stir-frying. If your wok doesn't come with a lid, they can be found in Chinese or other Asian stores.

When steaming or smoking in a wok, you'll need a steaming rack to suspend the food. Wok sets usually have them, but you can use any rack or metal trivet that fits comfortably in your wok.

Nothing beats a mesh strainer or 'spider' for scooping deep-fried foods from hot oil. They are also great for gently lowering raw food into the oil, without the risk of splashes.

ingredients

The following list is a quick guide to some of the distinctive ingredients commonly used in wok cooking. Most are readily available in supermarkets.

sauces and oils

Chinese rice wine Similar in flavour to a dry sherry, this rice wine is used mostly as a marinade or in sauces.

Fish sauce (nam pla) An extract of fermented fish, fish sauce has a less than appealing aroma yet its refreshingly salty taste makes it an essential seasoning throughout southeast

Asia. These days fish sauce is available in many supermarkets.

Hoisin sauce A thick, sweet, spicy sauce from China. Made from soya beans, vinegar, sugar, garlic, chilli and numerous spices. This sauce is delicious used in meat or seafood stir-fries or as a dipping sauce. Store in the fridge once opened.

Oyster sauce Oyster sauce is a thick, rich, brown Chinese sauce, made with extract of oysters. It's a great flavouring for stir-fries and adds a gorgeous, rich glaze to any dish. Store in the fridge once opened.

Sesame oil A rich nutty oil made from roasted white sesame seeds. Use sparingly. Its aroma is lost in high heats so add it to your stir-fries only at the end of the cooking.

Soy sauce Made from fermented soy beans, soy sauce is available in a variety of forms.

Light soy sauce is saltier than dark soy and is generally used to add flavour to marinades or in the first stages of stir-frying. The thicker, sweeter, dark soy sauce is mostly stirred in at the end of cooking to add richness and sweetness to the finished dish. It's also used as a dipping sauce.

herbs and spices

Five-spice powder An aromatic Chinese spice mixture made of ground star anise, fennel seeds, cloves, cinnamon and Szechuan pepper. More sweet and fragrant than spicy.

Ginger and galangal Fresh root ginger adds a fresh spiciness to many dishes in this book. Galangal is a member of the ginger family and although similar in appearance has a more floral, lemony flavour. It's an important ingredient in Thai curry pastes. If you cannot find galangal, use fresh root ginger instead. Store ginger and galangal in the fridge, wrapped in clingfilm, for up to 2 weeks.

Kaffir lime leaf Used in southeast Asian cooking, these little leaves add a refreshing zestiness to curries and stir-fries. Lime rind can be used as a substitute but you will lose out on the clean, fresh flavour.

Lemon grass A main ingredient in Thai and southeast Asian cuisines, lemon grass is a pale green stalk that is used whole or finely shredded in curry pastes. It is now readily available, but if you can't find it, you can replace it with a mixture of lime and lemon rind. It keeps in the fridge for about a week.

Szechuan peppercorns Not at all hot and actually not even peppercorns, Szechuan peppercorns are in fact the dried berries from a citrus shrub. They have a floral aroma and a very delicate spiciness. Available in most large supermarkets.

Tamarind The pulp from the fruit of the tamarind tree has a pungent, sour, lemony flavour and is frequently used in southeast Asian cooking.

Thai basil Also known as holy basil, this herb is similar in looks and fragrance to European basil. Thai basil leaves are slightly thicker and hairy, so they need to be cooked thoroughly. Thai basil is still mostly available only in Asian stores, so if you cannot find it you can replace it with European basil, which should be stirred into the recipe at the end of cooking.

menu suggestions

The dishes in this book can be cooked on their own and served with rice or noodles to provide a light lunch or supper. For a more filling meal, try combining two or more different dishes. Here are some ideas for combinations of wok-cooked dishes for different occasions.

simple weekday meals for 4

Minced Beef with Scrambled Eggs (page 28)
Mixed Vegetable Chop Suey (page 180)
Plain rice or noodles

Beef & Mixed Vegetable Sir-fry (page 18)
Egg Fried Rice (page 204)

Cashew Chicken with Peppers (page 76)
Pak Choi with Chilli & Ginger (page 174)
Plain rice or noodles

Stir-fried Sesame Chicken (page 110)
Vegetables in Yellow Bean Sauce
(page 188)

Pork with Black Bean & Chilli (page 54)
Mixed Vegetable Chop Suey (page 180)
Plain rice or noodles

simple vegetarian meals for 4

Vegetables with Sweet Chilli Sauce
(page 182)
Chilli Kale (page 194)
Egg Fried Rice (page 204)

Tofu Pad Thai (page 224), replacing the fish sauce with salt to taste and omitting the dried shrimp
Thai Yellow Vegetable Curry (page 168), replacing the fish sauce with salt to taste
Pak Choi with Chilli & Ginger (page 174)
Plain rice

entertaining menus for 4
Thai Beef with Peppers & Chilli (page 30)
Thai Green Chicken Curry (page 112)
Plain rice

Thai Red Pork & Bean Curry (page 68)
Seafood with Fresh Peppercorns (page 162)
Plain rice

Duck with Hoisin Sauce (page 106)
Prawns & Scallops with Asparagus (page 150)
Plain rice or noodles

vegetarian entertaining menu for 4
Tofu with Mushrooms (page 192), replacing the oyster sauce with dark soy sauce
Vegetables with Sweet Chilli Sauce (page 182)
Plain rice or noodles

entertaining menus for 6
Chinese Five-spice Spareribs (page 72)
Sweet & Sour Pork (page 48)
Chicken with Leek & Asparagus (page 86)
Singapore Noodles (page 232)
Chinese Pork & Prawn Fried Rice (page 208)

Pork, Chilli & Peanut Boats (page 58)
Mild Thai Fish Curry (page 158)
Thai Duck Jungle Curry (page 102)
Tofu Pad Thai (page 224)
Plain rice

seafood entertaining menu for 6
Salt & Pepper Squid (page 136)
Steamed Citrus Sea Bass (page 124)
Scallops in a Rich Szechuan Sauce (page 138)
Garlicky Choi Sum (page 178)
Plain rice

vegetarian entertaining menu for 6
Thai Yellow Vegetable Curry (page 168), replacing the fish sauce with salt to taste
Tofu with Chilli & Tamarind (page 198), omitting the shrimp paste
Stir-fried Asparagus & Mushrooms (page 170), replacing the oyster sauce with dark soy sauce
Aromatic Carrot & Mixed Nut Salad (page 184)
Plain rice

beef & lamb

beef & mixed vegetable stir-fry

Serves **4**

Preparation time **15 minutes**, plus marinating

Cooking time **12 minutes**

1 tablespoon **clear honey**

3 tablespoons **light soy sauce**

3 tablespoons **Chinese rice wine** or **dry sherry**

3 tablespoons **oyster sauce**

1 tablespoon **cornflour**

500 g (1 lb) **sirloin steak**, trimmed and cut into strips

50 ml (2 fl oz) **chicken stock**

½ teaspoon **white pepper**

3 tablespoons **groundnut oil**

1 teaspoon thinly chopped **fresh root ginger**

3 **garlic cloves**, finely chopped

125 g (4 oz) **broccoli florets**

150 g (5 oz) **shiitake mushrooms**, trimmed and halved, if large

2 **pak choi**, leaves separated

5 **spring onions**, thinly sliced

Mix together the honey, soy sauce, rice wine, oyster sauce and cornflour. Put the steak in a shallow, non-metallic dish and pour over half this mixture, then leave to marinate for at least 30 minutes. Stir the stock and white pepper into the remaining sauce mixture and set aside.

Heat 1 tablespoon of the oil in a wok over a high heat until the oil starts to shimmer. Add half the steak and stir-fry for about 2 minutes, then tip out on to a plate along with any juices. Heat another tablespoon of the oil and stir-fry the remaining steak in the same way.

Return the wok to the heat and wipe it clean with kitchen paper. Heat the remaining oil, then add the ginger and garlic. Add the broccoli and, after 30 seconds, the mushrooms. Stir-fry for 2 minutes, then add the pak choi, stir-frying until wilted.

Pour in the reserved sauce mixture and bring to the boil, then return the steak to the wok. Add the spring onions and stir until heated through. Serve immediately with rice, if liked.

For tofu with shiitake, pak choi & bean sprouts,

omit the beef and instead use half the sauce to marinate 300g (10 oz) cubed tofu for 10 minutes. Stir-fry in 3 tablespoons oil, then remove the tofu using a slotted spoon and continue the recipe as above, omitting the broccoli. Add 75 g (3 oz) bean sprouts to the wok together with the reserved sauce, then, once it's boiling, add the fried tofu and the spring onions.

crispy beef with carrots & orange

Serves **4**
Preparation time **10 minutes**
Cooking time **10 minutes**

2 teaspoons **Szechuan peppercorns**
pinch of **salt**
2 teaspoons **cornflour**
375 g (12 oz) thin **sirloin steaks**, trimmed and cut into thin strips
vegetable oil, for deep-frying
200 g (7 oz) **carrots**, cut into thin sticks
1 cm (½ inch) piece **fresh root ginger**, cut into thin strips
2 **garlic cloves**, finely chopped
3 tablespoons **light soy sauce**
3 tablespoons **orange juice**
finely grated rind of ½ **orange**
3 tablespoons **Chinese rice wine** or **dry sherry**
2 tablespoons **clear honey**

To garnish
3 **spring onions**, cut into thin strips
finely grated rind of ½ **orange**

Place the Szechuan peppercorns in a dry wok and stir over a medium heat until they begin to pop and release their aroma. Transfer to a pestle and mortar and pound with the salt until coarsely ground. Tip into a dish with the cornflour, add the beef strips and toss together.

Pour enough oil into the wok to deep-fry the carrots and beef, and heat it to 190°C (375°F), or until a cube of bread dropped into the oil turns golden in 20 seconds. Deep-fry the carrots for 2 minutes, until golden and crisp. They will look dry. Remove using a slotted spoon and drain on kitchen paper.

Deep-fry the beef in two batches for about 30 seconds, until crisp and unattractively dark, then remove using a slotted spoon and drain on kitchen paper.

Pour away all but 1 tablespoon of the oil and return the wok to the heat. Add the ginger and garlic and give them a good stir, then pour in the soy sauce, orange juice and rind and rice wine. (Reserve the other half of the orange rind for garnish.) Stir in the honey until it dissolves, then toss in the cooked beef and carrots and the spring onions. Stir over a low heat until the sauce becomes thick and sticky, then serve with steamed rice, if liked. Garnish with strips of spring onion and orange rind.

For crispy beef with broccoli, blanch 150 g (5 oz) small broccoli florets for 2 minutes in boiling water. Deep-fry the drained florets in place of the carrots, continuing with the recipe as above.

beef in black bean sauce

Serves **4**

Preparation time **10 minutes**

Cooking time **10 minutes**

3 tablespoons **groundnut oil**

500 g (1 lb) lean **beef**, cut
into thin slices

1 **red pepper**, cored,
deseeded and cut into strips

6 **baby sweetcorn**, cut in half
lengthways

1 **green chilli**, deseeded and
cut into strips

3 **shallots**, cut into thin
wedges

2 tablespoons **black bean
sauce**

4 tablespoons **water**

1 teaspoon **cornflour** mixed
to a paste with 1 tablespoon
water

salt

Heat 1 tablespoon of the oil in a wok over a high
heat until the oil starts to shimmer. Add half the
beef, season with salt and stir-fry for 2 minutes.
When it begins to colour, lift the beef on to a plate
using a slotted spoon. Heat another 1 tablespoon
of the oil and stir-fry the rest of the beef in the
same way.

Return the wok to the heat and wipe it clean with
kitchen paper. Heat the remaining oil and tip in the
pepper, sweetcorn, chilli and shallots. Stir-fry for
2 minutes before adding the black bean sauce, the
measurement water and the cornflour paste. Bring
to the boil, return the beef to the wok and stir-fry
until the sauce thickens and coats the stir-fry in
a velvety glaze. Serve with rice, if liked.

For king prawns with spring onions & black bean
sauce, replace the beef with 250 g (8 oz) raw peeled
king prawns. Replace the sweetcorn, green chilli and
shallots with 75 g (3 oz) bean sprouts, 1 red chilli
and 3 spring onions cut into 1 cm (½ inch) pieces,
and cook as above.

spiced beef & vegetable stew

Serves **4**
Preparation time **15 minutes**
Cooking time **2½ hours**

2 tablespoons **rapeseed** or
  olive oil
1 large **onion**, chopped
1 tablespoon chopped **fresh
  root ginger**
2 **chillies**, sliced
500 g (1 lb) lean **braising** or
  stewing steak, cut into
  2.5 cm (1 inch) cubes
2 **garlic cloves**, crushed
600 ml (1 pint) **beef stock**
5 **star anise**
1 teaspoon **Chinese
  five-spice powder**
1 **cinnamon stick**
1 teaspoon **fennel seeds**
2 **dried kaffir lime leaves**
1 **lemon grass stalk**, chopped
1 teaspoon **black peppercorns**
2 tablespoons **shoyu** or
  tamari sauce
400 g (13 oz) **carrots**, cut into
  1 cm (½ inch) slices
500 g (1 lb) **mooli** or **turnips**,
  cut into 1 cm (½ inch) slices
Chinese chives or **regular
  chives**, to garnish

Heat the oil in a wok over a medium heat. Add the
onion, ginger and chillies and stir-fry for 5–7 minutes.

Turn the heat up to high, add the beef and stir-fry for
5–10 minutes until lightly browned, stirring occasionally.

Add the garlic, stock, star anise, Chinese five-spice
powder, cinnamon, fennel seeds, lime leaves, lemon
grass, peppercorns and shoyu sauce and stir well.
Bring the mixture back to the boil, then turn the heat
down, cover the pan and simmer gently for 1½ hours,
stirring occasionally. Add the carrots and mooli and
continue cooking, covered, for another 45 minutes
or until the vegetables have softened.

Skim any fat off the surface and garnish with the
chives before serving.

For sesame broccoli, to accompany the stew, blanch
500 g (1 lb) broccoli florets in a saucepan of boiling
water for 2 minutes, then drain and place on a serving
dish. Make a dressing by combining 1 teaspoon
sesame oil, 1 tablespoon shoyu sauce and 1 crushed
garlic clove, and pour it over the broccoli. Just before
serving, sprinkle the dish with 1 tablespoon toasted
sesame seeds.

hot thai beef salad

Serves **4**

Preparation time **15 minutes**

Cooking time **5–10 minutes**

2 tablespoons **vegetable oil**

500 g (1 lb) **rump** or **fillet steak**, cut across the grain into thin strips

3 **garlic cloves**, finely chopped

2 **green chillies**, finely sliced into rings

juice of 2 **lemons**

1 tablespoon **Thai fish sauce (nam pla)**

2 teaspoons **caster sugar**

2 ripe **papayas**, finely sliced

½ large **cucumber**, cut into matchsticks

75 g (3 oz) **bean sprouts**

1 head crisp **lettuce**, shredded

Heat the oil in a wok over a moderate heat. Add the steak, garlic and chillies, increase the heat to high and stir-fry for 3–4 minutes or until the steak is browned on all sides.

Pour in the lemon juice and fish sauce, add the sugar and stir-fry until sizzling, then remove the wok from the heat.

Remove the steak from the liquid using a slotted spoon and toss together with the papayas, cucumber, bean sprouts and lettuce. Drizzle the liquid from the wok over the salad ingredients as a dressing and serve hot with a bowl of chilli sauce, if liked.

For Thai beef salad with mango, cook the beef with the garlic, chillies, lemon juice, fish sauce and sugar as above. Substitute the papayas for 2 ripe, finely sliced mangoes and omit the lettuce. Toss the beef with the mangoes, cucumber and bean sprouts and serve hot on a bed of coriander leaves instead of lettuce, drizzled with the liquid from the wok.

minced beef with scrambled eggs

Serves **4**

Preparation time **5 minutes**,
    plus marinating

Cooking time **10 minutes**

300 g (10 oz) **minced beef**

1½ tablespoons **light soy
    sauce**

3 teaspoons **sesame oil**

1 tablespoon **Chinese rice
    wine** or **dry sherry**

1 teaspoon **caster sugar**

½ teaspoon **salt**

3 tablespoons **groundnut oil**

1 **red onion**, cut into thin
    wedges

1 **red chilli**, deseeded and
    finely chopped

3 **eggs**

black pepper

handful of **coriander leaves**,
    to garnish

Break up the beef with a fork and place it in a bowl
with 1 tablespoon of the soy sauce, 2 teaspoons of the
sesame oil and the rice wine. Stir in the sugar and salt
and season with a generous grinding of black pepper.
Leave to marinate for 15 minutes.

Heat 2 tablespoons groundnut oil in a wok over a high
heat until the oil starts to shimmer. Add the onion and
chilli and stir-fry for 2 minutes, until it begins to colour.
Add the beef and let the meat cook until it becomes
golden but not browned. Drain in a sieve.

Wipe the wok clean, return it to the heat and pour in
the remaining groundnut oil. While it heats up again,
combine the eggs, remaining soy sauce and sesame
oil and season lightly with freshly ground black pepper.
Tip the mixture into the hot oil and scramble for about
1 minute until mostly set, but still moist and creamy.
Return the cooked beef to the wok and stir-fry for
1 minute. Scatter with coriander and serve with rice,
if liked.

For minced chicken with egg & noodles, soak
200 g (7 oz) thick dried rice noodles according to
the packet instructions, drain and set aside. Use
300 g (10 oz) minced chicken instead of beef and
cook with the other stir-fried ingredients as above.
Add the drained noodles to the work when returning
the mince. Stir-fry until hot, then stir in the coriander
and the juice of 1 lime.

thai beef with peppers & chilli

Serves **4**
Preparation time **5 minutes**
Cooking time **15 minutes**

2 tablespoons **groundnut oil**
2 **sirloin steaks**, about 250 g
　(8 oz) each
1 **onion**, sliced
1 each **red, yellow and green
　pepper**, cored, deseeded
　and cut into thick strips
1 **lemon grass stalk**, finely
　chopped
2 **red chillies**, deseeded and
　finely chopped
2 **garlic cloves**, finely
　chopped
1 cm (½ inch) piece **fresh root
　ginger**, finely chopped
4 tablespoons **oyster sauce**
3 tablespoons **water**
handful of **Thai basil leaves**
salt and **black pepper**

Rub 1 tablespoon of the oil over the steaks and season them with salt and freshly ground black pepper. Cook them in a hot griddle pan for 3 minutes on each side, then set them aside to rest for 3–4 minutes. Slice into thin strips.

Heat the rest of the oil in a wok over a high heat until the oil starts to shimmer, then add the onion. After 3 minutes, when it starts to soften, add the peppers, lemon grass, chillies, garlic and ginger. Then add the oyster sauce and measurement water and bring to the boil.

Remove from the heat and fold in the basil and reserved steak strips. Serve immediately.

For fragrant Thai beef, pepper & chilli salad, cook 50 g (2 oz) thin dried rice noodles according to the packet instructions. Drain, refresh and set aside. Cook the beef and peppers as above and allow to cool. Tip into a bowl and add the basil, a handful of toasted cashew nuts, a handful of coriander leaves and the rice noodles, and toss together.

thai red beef curry

Serves **4**

Preparation time **5 minutes**

Cooking time **8 minutes**

1 tablespoon **groundnut oil**

625 g (1¼ lb) **sirloin steak**,
trimmed and thinly sliced

2 tablespoons **ready-made** or
**homemade Thai red curry
paste** (see page 80)

400 ml (14 fl oz) can **coconut
milk**

150 ml (¼ pint) **beef** or
vegetable stock

1 tablespoon **demerara sugar**

2.5 cm (1 inch) piece **fresh
root ginger**, thickly sliced

1 **lemon grass stalk**, bruised

100 g (3½ oz) **mangetout**,
diagonally sliced

100 g (3½ oz) **beansprouts**

1 tablespoon **Thai fish sauce
(nam pla)**

grated rind of 1 **lime**

small handful of **coriander
leaves**

Heat the oil in a wok over a high heat until the oil
starts to simmer. Add the steak and curry paste, stirring
to coat the beef, and stir-fry for about 2 minutes, until
the beef is lightly golden but still pink in the middle.

Pour in the coconut milk and stock and add the
sugar, ginger, lemon grass, mangetout, beansprouts,
fish sauce and lime rind. Bring to the boil, then reduce
the heat and simmer for 2 minutes, until the mangetout
are tender.

Remove the ginger and lemon grass from the curry
and stir in the coriander. Serve with rice, if liked.

For Thai red vegetable curry, omit the beef and
replace with a cubed aubergine, 6 baby sweetcorn,
cut lengthways, and 25g (1 oz) drained canned sliced
bamboo shoots. Fry the curry paste in the oil for
1 minute, then add the vegetables and other
ingredients as above. Simmer for 7–8 minutes,
until the aubergine is tender.

indonesian beef strips

Serves **4**

Preparation time **5 minutes**

Cooking time **8 minutes**

1 **onion**, roughly chopped

2 **garlic cloves**

2.5 cm (1 inch) piece **fresh root ginger**, sliced

1 **red chilli**, deseeded

2 tablespoons **dried shrimp**

3 tablespoons **groundnut oil**

500 g (1 lb) lean **beef**, cut into thin strips

1 tablespoon **tamarind paste**

2 tablespoons **dark soy sauce**

4 tablespoons **water**

1 teaspoon **demerara sugar**

small handful of shredded **mint leaves**, plus extra whole ones to garnish

1 tablespoon snipped **chives**, to garnish

Blend the onion, garlic, ginger, chilli and dried shrimp in a food processor until it forms a smooth paste.

Heat the oil in a wok over a medium heat and cook the paste, stirring constantly, for about 2 minutes, until the oil separates from the other ingredients.

Add the beef and stir-fry until the meat becomes opaque, then add the tamarind paste, soy sauce and water. Simmer, uncovered, for 2–3 minutes, until most of the liquid has evaporated and the meat is tender. Stir in the sugar and shredded mint leaves, season to taste and garnish with chives and a few whole mint leaves. Serve with a vegetable dish and rice, if liked.

For pork with yellow peppers & mushrooms, replace the beef with 500 g (1 lb) pork strips, cut into thin strips, and add 1 yellow pepper, cored and cut into thin strips, and 75g (3 oz) halved chestnut mushrooms. Follow the recipe as above, adding the additional vegetables to the wok with the meat.

korean beef with cucumber

Serves **4**

Preparation time **12 minutes**,
  plus marinating

Cooking time **10 minutes**

500 g (1 lb) **sirloin steak**,
  trimmed and cut into thin
  strips

2 teaspoons **sesame oil**

2 tablespoons **light soy
  sauce**

½ teaspoon **salt**

1 teaspoon **caster sugar**

2 **garlic cloves**, crushed

1 tablespoon chopped **fresh
  root ginger**

1 **cucumber**

3 tablespoons **groundnut oil**

4 **spring onions**, finely sliced
  on the diagonal

2 tablespoons toasted
  sesame seeds, to garnish

Marinate the beef for 30 minutes in a bowl with the
sesame oil, soy sauce, salt, sugar, garlic and ginger.

Peel the cucumber, cut it in half lengthways and then
into 1cm (½ inch) slices.

Heat half the oil in a wok over a high heat until the
oil starts to shimmer. Add half the beef and stir-fry
for 2–3 minutes, until just cooked, then remove using
a slotted spoon. Heat the remaining oil and stir-fry
the rest of the beef in the same way.

Add the cucumber and spring onions. Stir-fry for
1 more minute, until the cucumber is only slightly
tender, and serve garnished with a scattering of
toasted sesame seeds.

For spiced pork with cucumber, replace the
beef with 500 g (1 lb) lean pork, cut into strips.
Add 1 tablespoon crushed coriander seeds to the
marinade ingredients and prepare the dish as above.
Finish by tossing 1 red chilli, cut into thin rounds, a
handful of coriander leaves and the juice of ½ lime
into the finished dish.

beef with yellow peppers

Serves **4**

Preparation time **10 minutes**

Cooking time **8 minutes**

½ tablespoon **groundnut oil**

1 tablespoon **black bean sauce**

400 g (13 oz) **rump** or **fillet steak**, sliced

1 **red chilli**, deseeded and cut into strips

100 g (3½ oz) **onion**, cut into squares

300 g (10 oz) **yellow peppers**, cored, deseeded and cut into squares

200 ml (7 fl oz) hot **beef stock**

1 teaspoon **cornflour** mixed to a paste with 1 tablespoon **water**

Heat the oil in a wok over a high heat until the oil starts to shimmer. Add the black bean sauce and stir-fry for a few seconds, then add the sliced beef and stir-fry for about 1 minute until half-cooked.

Mix in the chilli, onion and yellow peppers and stir-fry for 1–2 minutes. Then add the hot stock and bring to the boil.

Stir in the cornflour paste slowly until the sauce has thickened and become transparent. Serve immediately.

For spicy tomato dip, to serve with the beef, heat 100 ml (3½ fl oz) passata in a wok with 2 tablespoons Chinese rice wine, 1 tablespoon light soy sauce, 1 teaspoon chilli oil and 2 tablespoons water. Simmer until reduced to a thick sauce, then set aside to cool before serving.

beef, tomato & onion salad

Serves **4**
Preparation time **10 minutes**
Cooking time **6 minutes**

2 tablespoons **groundnut oil**
1 tablespoon finely chopped
  fresh root ginger
2 **garlic cloves**, finely
  chopped
375 g (12 oz) **sirloin steak**,
  trimmed and cut into thin
  strips
250 g (8 oz) **cherry**
  tomatoes, halved
handful of **coriander leaves**
1 **red onion**, thinly sliced

Sauce
1 tablespoon **dark soy sauce**
2 teaspoons **cornflour**
1 tablespoon **Chinese rice**
  wine or **dry sherry**
pinch of **salt**

Combine the sauce ingredients in a bowl, stirring well
to remove any lumps. Set aside.

Heat the oil in a wok over a high heat until the oil starts
to shimmer. Add the ginger and garlic and stir-fry for
a few seconds, then tip in the beef and continue stir-
frying for 2–3 minutes until the meat is lightly browned.

Add the sauce ingredients, stir the mixture thoroughly
and cook until reduced to a thick glaze. Tip the beef
into a bowl with the remaining ingredients. Check the
seasoning and serve as a warm salad.

For chicken salad with mint & crunchy vegetables,
omit the beef and cook 375 g (12 oz) chicken breast
strips in the garlic and ginger as above. Stir in the
sauce and, when the chicken is cooked through and
well glazed, toss into a bowl with 4 thinly sliced
radishes, 50 g (2 oz) bean sprouts, 50 g (2 oz)
sliced sugar snap peas and a generous handful
of mint leaves.

lamb with sugar snap peas

Serves **4**

Preparation time **10 minutes**, plus marinating

Cooking time **10 minutes**

2 teaspoons **cornflour**

1½ tablespoons **Chinese rice wine** or **dry sherry**

2 tablespoons **light soy sauce**

2 **garlic cloves**, finely chopped

500g (1 lb) lean **lamb steaks**, cut into thin slices

1 teaspoon **Szechuan peppercorns**

¼ teaspoon **rock salt**

3 tablespoons **groundnut oil**

75 g (3 oz) **sugar snap peas**, sliced into 3

1 teaspoon **sesame oil**

1 **red chilli**, deseeded and finely chopped

1 **spring onion**, very finely shredded

Combine the cornflour with the rice wine to make a paste, then stir in the soy sauce and garlic. Add the lamb and stir to cover, then leave to marinate for 25–30 minutes. Drain.

Place the Szechuan peppercorns in a dry wok and stir over a medium heat until they begin to pop and release their aroma. Transfer to a pestle and mortar and pound with the salt until coarsely ground.

Heat half the oil in a wok over a high heat until the oil starts to shimmer. Add half the lamb and stir-fry for 3 minutes, then remove using a slotted spoon. Heat the remaining oil and stir-fry the rest of the lamb in the same way.

Return all the lamb to the wok, add the sugar snaps and after 1 minute stir in the sesame oil, chilli, spring onion and the ground salt and pepper mixture. Cook for 1 more minute, then serve with noodles, if liked.

For scallops with mangetout & Szechuan pepper,

replace the lamb with 12 prepared scallops and the sugar snaps with 75 g (3 oz) halved mangetout. Marinate the scallops as above, then stir-fry in 2 batches of 6 scallops. Return to the wok, add the mangetout and other ingredients, and continue as above.

lamb with sweet potatoes & beans

Serves **4**

Preparation time **15 minutes**

Cooking time **15 minutes**

3 tablespoons **groundnut oil**

2.5 cm (1 inch) piece **fresh root ginger**, finely chopped

2 **garlic cloves**, finely chopped

2 **red chillies**, deseeded and cut into strips

400 g (13 oz) **sweet potato**, peeled, thinly sliced and slices halved

150 g (5 oz) **French beans**, cut in half

250 g (8 oz) lean **lamb steaks**, cut into thin strips

3 tablespoons **oyster sauce**

1 tablespoon **water**

1 teaspoon **sesame oil**

Heat half the oil in a wok over a high heat until the oil starts to shimmer. Add the ginger, garlic and chillies and stir-fry for a few seconds before adding the sweet potato. Stir-fry for 3 minutes, add the French beans and stir-fry for a further 3–4 minutes, until the sweet potato is tender and the beans are golden. Tip the vegetables on to a large plate and set aside while you cook the lamb.

Return the wok to the heat, wipe it clean with some kitchen paper and heat the remaining groundnut oil. Add the lamb and stir-fry for 2 minutes, then stir in the oyster sauce and measurement water. Cook, stirring, for 1 minute, then toss in the cooked vegetables and stir-fry for a final minute. Pour in the sesame oil, stir well to combine and serve.

For chicken with carrots & black bean sauce, slice 250 g (8 oz) carrots and use in the recipe instead of the sweet potatoes. Replace the lamb with 250 g (8 oz) cubed chicken breast and use 3 tablespoons black bean sauce instead of the oyster sauce.

pork

sweet & sour pork

Serves **4**
Preparation time **15 minutes**,
  plus marinating
Cooking time **20 minutes**

4 tablespoons **cornflour**
1 tablespoon **Chinese rice wine**
1 tablespoon **light soy sauce**
2 teaspoons **sesame oil**
1 **egg yolk**
½ teaspoon **salt**
500 g (1 lb) lean **pork**, trimmed,
  cut in 2.5 cm (1 inch) pieces
1 **red** and 1 **green pepper**,
  deseeded and cubed
1 **carrot**, sliced into rounds
150 g (5 oz) drained **tinned
  pineapple**, chopped
2 tablespoons **light soy sauce**
4 **spring onions**, sliced
4 tablespoons **plain flour**
vegetable oil, for deep-frying

Sweet & sour sauce
200 ml (7 fl oz) **malt vinegar**
100 ml (3½ fl oz) **Chinese
  rice wine**
2 tablespoons **caster sugar**
4 tablespoons **tomato purée**
1.5 cm (1 inch) piece **fresh
  ginger**, sliced
3 **garlic cloves**, crushed

Place 1 tablespoon of the cornflour in a large bowl
and stir in the rice wine to make a paste, then stir in
the soy sauce, sesame oil, egg yolk and salt. Add the
pork and mix well, then cover and leave to marinate
for 2 hours or up to overnight in the refrigerator.

Stir the ingredients for the sweet and sour sauce in a
pan and bring to the boil. Add the peppers and carrot
and reduce the heat. Simmer gently for 5 minutes, stir
in the pineapple and cook for a further 3–4 minutes
until the vegetables and fruit are tender. Stir in the soy
sauce and spring onions and set aside.

Combine the flour and remaining 3 tablespoons of
cornflour and stir into the marinated pork.

Pour enough oil into the wok to deep-fry the pork,
and heat it to 190°C (375°F), or until a cube of bread
dropped into the oil turns golden in 20 seconds. Deep-
fry the pork in batches for 3–4 minutes, until golden.
Remove using a slotted spoon and drain on kitchen
paper, then toss into the sweet and sour sauce. Serve
with rice, if liked.

For sweet & sour vegetables, omit the pork and
marinade. Make the sweet and sour sauce as above
and set aside. Heat 1 tablespoon groundnut oil in
a wok and stir-fry 1 sliced carrot, 1 red and 1 yellow
red pepper, deseeded and cut into strips, 200 g
(7 oz) cauliflower florets and 5 sliced spring onions,
for 3 minutes. Pour in the sauce and simmer until the
vegetables are tender.

thai red pork curry

Serves **4**
Preparation time **20 minutes**
Cooking time **30 minutes**

2 tablespoons **groundnut oil**
2 **shallots**, finely sliced
1 **green chilli**, deseeded and
  sliced
2 tablespoons **ready-made** or
  **homemade Thai red curry
  paste** (see page 80)
500 g (1 lb) lean **pork**, sliced
1 tablespoon **Thai fish sauce
  (nam pla)**
½ teaspoon **soft brown sugar**
150 ml (¼ pint) canned
  coconut milk
75 g (3 oz) canned sliced
  bamboo shoots, drained,
  plus extra to serve
2 tablespoons chopped
  coriander leaves

To garnish
red chilli, sliced into rings
coriander sprigs

Heat the oil in a wok over a gentle heat. Add the shallots and chilli and stir-fry for 3 minutes, then add the curry paste and fry for 1 more minute.

Stir in the pork, coating the pieces evenly in the spice mixture, then add the fish sauce and brown sugar and stir-fry for another 3 minutes. Pour in the coconut milk and bring the curry to the boil, then reduce the heat and simmer gently for 20 minutes, stirring occasionally, until the pork is tender.

Stir in the bamboo shoots and chopped coriander and cook for a final 2 minutes, to heat through.

Garnish the curry with the red chilli slices and the coriander sprigs, and serve immediately with more bamboo shoots.

For mild Thai yellow curry, omit the green chilli and replace the curry paste with 2 tablespoons ready-made or homemade Thai yellow curry paste (see page 148). Increase the coconut milk to 400 ml (14 fl oz) and when adding it to the pan, also stir in 200 g (7 oz) sliced new potatoes. Otherwise, complete the recipe as above.

pork with chilli & basil

Serves **4**

Preparation time **10 minutes**

Cooking time **8–10 minutes**

2 tablespoons **vegetable oil**

1 **garlic clove**, crushed

2 **red chillies**, finely chopped,
  or to taste

125 g (4 oz) lean **pork**, finely
  sliced

¼ teaspoon **black pepper**

1 tablespoon **Thai fish sauce
  (nam pla)**

½ teaspoon **sugar**

50 g (2 oz) canned sliced
  bamboo shoots, drained
  (optional)

2 tablespoons finely chopped
  onion

½ **red pepper**, cored,
  deseeded and finely sliced

4 tablespoons **chicken** or
  vegetable stock

2 handfuls of **basil leaves**,
  plus extra to garnish

3–4 large **red chillies**, sliced
  and deseeded, to garnish

Heat the oil in a wok over a high heat. Add the garlic
and chillies to the wok and stir-fry until the garlic is
just golden. Add the pork, pepper, fish sauce and sugar,
stirring constantly.

Stir in the bamboo shoots, if using, with the onion, red
pepper and stock. Cook for 5 minutes. Stir in the basil
leaves and cook for 1 minute more.

Garnish with basil leaves and large slices of red chilli,
then serve immediately with rice, if liked.

For steak with chilli & basil, substitute 125 g (4 oz)
rump steak for the pork and marinate it in 1 tablespoon
ready-made or homemade Thai red curry paste
(see page 80) for 30 minutes before following the
recipe as above.

pork with black bean & chilli

Serves **4**

Preparation time **15 minutes**, plus marinating

Cooking time **12 minutes**

1 teaspoon **cornflour**

2 tablespoons **Chinese rice wine** or **dry sherry**

1 teaspoon **sugar**

½ teaspoon **salt**

2 tablespoons **black bean sauce**

500 g (1 lb) lean **pork**, trimmed and cut into long, thin strips

3 tablespoons **groundnut oil**

1 small **red onion**, sliced

1 **red pepper**, cored, deseeded and sliced

1.5 cm (¾ inch) piece **fresh root ginger**, cut into matchsticks

2 **garlic cloves**, finely chopped

2 tablespoons **water**

4 **spring onions**, thinly sliced

2 **red chillies**, deseeded and thinly sliced

2 teaspoons **sesame oil**

Put the cornflour, rice wine, sugar, salt and black bean sauce in a large bowl and combine to make a smooth paste. Toss the pork into the bowl and stir to cover. Set aside for 10 minutes.

Heat 1 tablespoon of the groundnut oil in a wok over a high heat until the oil starts to shimmer. Add half the pork and stir-fry for 2–3 minutes until golden, then remove with a slotted spoon and set aside. Heat another 1 tablespoon of oil and stir-fry the rest of the pork in the same way.

Wipe the wok clean with a piece of kitchen paper and heat the remaining oil over a high heat. Add the onion, red pepper, ginger and garlic and stir-fry for 2 minutes. Return the pork to the wok with the measurement water and stir-fry for 1 minute.

Add the spring onions, chillies and sesame oil to the wok and cook for a further 30 seconds, then serve.

For monkfish & mushrooms with black bean sauce, cut 500 g (1 lb) monkfish into chunks and use in place of the pork. Trim 200 g (7 oz) shiitake mushrooms and use them instead of the red pepper, otherwise follow the recipe as above.

pork with brown rice

Serves **4**

Preparation time **15 minutes**

Cooking time **30 minutes**

200 g (7 oz) **long-grain brown rice**

1 tablespoon **sunflower oil**

400 g (13 oz) lean **pork**, thinly sliced, large slices halved crossways

2 **garlic cloves**, finely chopped

300 g (10 oz) **vegetables** for stir-frying, such as strips of pepper, bean sprouts, broccoli florets, sliced leeks and carrot sticks

350 ml (12 fl oz) **pressed apple juice**

2 teaspoons **tomato purée**

1 teaspoon **Chinese five-spice powder**

Bring a saucepan of water to the boil, add the brown rice and simmer for 30 minutes.

Just before the rice is cooked, heat the oil in a wok over a high heat until the oil starts to shimmer. Add the pork and garlic and fry, stirring, over a high heat for 3 minutes. Add the vegetables and stir-fry for 3 minutes.

Mix the apple juice with the tomato purée and Chinese five-spice powder, pour the mixture into the wok and cook for 1 minute.

Drain the rice, spoon it into serving bowls and top with the pork stir-fry.

For brown rice with prawns, red onion & peppers, replace the pork with 250 g (8 oz) raw peeled king prawns and stir-fry with the garlic for 1 minute. Add 1 each finely chopped red and green peppers and 1 finely sliced red onion, then complete the recipe as above.

pork, chilli & peanut boats

Serves **4** as a starter
Preparation time **5 minutes**
Cooking time **10 minutes**

1 tablespoon **groundnut oil**
2 **garlic cloves**, finely
  chopped
1 large **dried chilli**, deseeded
  and chopped
200 g (7 oz) **minced pork**
40 g (1½ oz) **French beans**,
  cut into 1 cm (½ inch)
  lengths
1 tablespoon **Thai fish sauce
  (nam pla)**
30 g (¾ oz) **roasted peanuts**,
  roughly chopped
1 tablespoon **water**
2 tablespoons **light soy
  sauce**
¼ teaspoon **caster sugar**
8 **little gem leaves**
sweet chilli sauce, to serve

Heat the oil in a large wok over a medium heat until
the oil starts to shimmer. Add the garlic and dried chilli
and stir quickly for a few seconds. Add the minced
pork and stir-fry for 4–5 minutes until the meat has
become golden.

Add the French beans and cook for 1 minute, then add
the fish sauce, peanuts, measurement water, soy sauce
and sugar and cook for 1 more minute. Spoon into the
lettuce leaves and serve with some sweet chilli sauce
on the side.

For noodles with minced beef & spring onion,

follow the first stage of the recipe, using 200 g (7 oz)
beef instead of pork, then replace the beans with
4 spring onions cut into thin rounds. Stir the finished
dish into 200 g (7 oz) cooked egg noodles, adding
½ teaspoon sesame oil and a further 2 tablespoons
light soy sauce.

szechuan pork with tofu

Serves **4**
Preparation time **5 minutes**
Cooking time **15 minutes**

¼ teaspoon **Szechuan peppercorns**
½ teaspoon coarse **sea salt**
250 g (8½ oz) firm **tofu**
vegetable oil, for deep-frying
2 tablespoons **groundnut oil**
3 **garlic cloves**, finely chopped
1 tablespoon chopped **fresh root ginger**
300 g (10 oz) **minced pork**
4 tablespoons **Chinese rice wine** or **dry sherry**
1 tablespoon **caster sugar**
1 tablespoon **oyster sauce**
2 tablespoons **light soy sauce**
1 teaspoon **sesame oil**
1 tablespoon **malt vinegar**
½ teaspoon **chilli oil**
4 tablespoons **chicken stock** or **water**
3 baby **leeks**, trimmed, cleaned and diagonally sliced
1 **red chilli**, deseeded and thinly sliced, to garnish

Place the Szechuan peppercorns in a dry wok and stir over a medium heat until they begin to pop and release their aroma. Transfer to a pestle and mortar and pound with the salt until coarsely ground. Set aside.

Drain the tofu and pat it dry with kitchen paper before cutting it into 20 equal-sized cubes. Pour enough oil into the wok to deep-fry the tofu, and heat it to 190°C (375°F), or until a cube of bread dropped into the oil turns golden in 20 seconds. Add half the tofu and deep-fry until puffy and golden, then remove using a slotted spoon and drain on kitchen paper. Stir-fry the remaining tofu in the same way and set aside. Drain all the oil from the wok and wipe clean with kitchen paper.

Heat the groundnut oil in a wok over a high heat until the oil starts to shimmer. Add the garlic and ginger and stir until golden. Tip in the pork and stir-fry for about 2 minutes until opaque but not golden. Add the prepared ground salt and peppercorns, the rice wine, sugar, oyster and soy sauces, sesame oil, malt vinegar, chilli oil, stock and leeks. Gently slide in the tofu, keeping the pieces separate in the wok, and reduce the heat to a gentle simmer. Heat through for 3 minutes and serve with a scattering of sliced chilli.

For spiced pork with lettuce & noodles, follow the recipe as above, replacing the tofu with 250 g (8 oz) cooked thin egg noodles. Top with 2 quartered tomatoes, 4 sliced spring onions and a handful of thinly shredded iceburg lettuce and serve.

pork & chinese leaves with chilli

Serves **4**

Preparation time **5 minutes**

Cooking time **8 minutes**

2 tablespoons **groundnut oil**

2 **garlic cloves**, finely chopped

1 tablespoon chopped **fresh root ginger**

300 g (10 oz) **minced pork**

200 g (7 oz) **Chinese leaves**, shredded

3 tablespoons **Chinese rice wine** or **dry sherry**

2 tablespoons **oyster sauce**

1 teaspoon **caster sugar**

1 teaspoon **sesame oil**

1 **red chilli**, deseeded and thinly sliced, to garnish

Heat the oil in a wok over a high heat until the oil starts to shimmer. Add the garlic and ginger and stir quickly for a few seconds. Add the pork and stir-fry for 2–3 minutes until the meat has become opaque but not golden.

Add the Chinese leaves and cook for 1 minute, then add the rice wine, oyster sauce and sugar and stir-fry for 2 minutes until the Chinese leaves are just tender. Stir in the sesame oil and cook for 30 seconds, then serve with a scattering of sliced chilli.

For pork & Chinese leaves soup, fry the garlic and ginger as above. Pour in the rice wine, sugar and 2 tablespoons light soy sauce and simmer for 1 minute. Add 1 litre (1¾ pints) chicken stock and bring to the boil, then stir in the pork, Chinese leaves and chilli. Simmer gently for 10 minutes and serve with a scattering of shredded spring onions.

pork with ginger, coriander & soy

Serves **4**

Preparation time **15 minutes**, plus marinating

Cooking time **10 minutes**

1 tablespoon **coriander seeds**

2 tablespoons finely chopped **fresh root ginger**

2 **garlic cloves**, finely chopped

2 **green chillies**, deseeded and finely chopped

½ small **onion**, finely sliced

1 tablespoon **clear honey**

2 tablespoons **dark soy sauce**

½ teaspoon **salt**

500 g (1 lb) lean **pork**, cut into 1.5 cm (¾ inch) cubes

4 tablespoons **vegetable oil**

1 large **carrot**, thinly sliced

6 **spring onions**, cut into 1.5 cm (¾ inch) lengths

juice of 1 **lime**

Place the coriander seeds in a wok over a medium heat and stir them gently for 30 seconds, or until they begin to release their aroma. Remove and pound using a pestle and mortar until coarsely ground.

Place the ground coriander in a large bowl with the ginger, garlic, chillies, onion, honey, soy sauce, salt and pork and stir well to combine. Cover and leave to marinate for 2 hours or up to overnight in the refrigerator. Drain the pork, reserving the marinade, and pat the meat dry with kitchen paper.

Heat half the oil in a wok over a high heat until the oil starts to shimmer. Tip in half the pork and stir-fry for 2–3 minutes until browned, then transfer to a plate. Wipe the wok clean with a piece of kitchen paper and return to the heat. Heat the remaining oil and stir-fry the rest of the pork in the same way.

Return all the meat to the wok and add the carrot and half the spring onions. Stir-fry for 1 minute, pour in the reserved marinade and stir until the sauce comes to the boil and coats the pork. Squeeze the lime juice over the mixture, toss in the remaining spring onions and serve with noodles, if liked.

For prawns with courgette, ginger & coriander, replace the pork with 250 g (8 oz) peeled raw king prawns and the carrot with 1 large courgette, sliced. Follow the recipe as above and finish the dish by tossing in a handful of coriander leaves.

pork with honey & ginger

Serves **4**

Preparation time **10 minutes**, plus marinating

Cooking time **10 minutes**

500 g (1 lb) lean **pork**, thinly sliced

1 teaspoon **cornflour**

2 teaspoons finely chopped **fresh root ginger**

2 tablespoons **dark soy sauce**

2 tablespoons **honey**

2 tablespoons **Chinese rice wine** or **dry sherry**

2 teaspoons **Chinese five-spice powder**

1 teaspoon **sesame oil**

3 tablespoons **groundnut oil**

1 **green pepper**, cored, deseeded and cubed

3 **spring onions**, cut into 5 cm (2 inch) lengths

1 tablespoon **malt vinegar**

1 tablespoon **light soy sauce**

2 tablespoons **water**

salt and **white pepper**

squeeze of **lime juice**

Put the pork in a bowl and sprinkle in the cornflour. Add the ginger, dark soy sauce, honey, rice wine, Chinese five-spice powder and sesame oil. Cover and leave to marinate for 30 minutes or up to overnight in the refrigerator.

Heat half the groundnut oil in a wok over a high heat until the oil starts to shimmer. Drain the pork and add half the meat to the wok. Stir-fry for 2 minutes, then remove using a slotted spoon. Wipe the wok clean with a piece of kitchen paper. Heat the remaining oil and stir-fry the rest of the pork in the same way.

Return the reserved pork to the wok, add the pepper, spring onions, vinegar, light soy sauce and measurement water and stir-fry for a further 3 minutes until the pork is coloured and the peppers have softened slightly. Add salt and freshly ground white pepper to taste, then a squeeze of lime. Serve with rice and lime wedges, if liked.

For mussels with honey & ginger, omit the pork and cornflour and instead use 1 kg (2 lb) cleaned live mussels. Heat 1 tablespoon groundnut oil in a wok. Add the ginger and stir for a few seconds, then add the dark soy sauce, honey, rice wine and sesame oil. Bring to the boil, tip in the mussels (discarding any open ones that do not close when tapped) and simmer, covered, for 2–3 minutes, until opened. (Discard any that do not open.) Stir in the spring onions, light soy sauce and lime juice and serve.

thai red pork & bean curry

Serves **4**

Preparation time **10 minutes**

Cooking time **5 minutes**

2 tablespoons **groundnut oil**

1½ tablespoons **ready-made** or **homemade Thai red curry paste** (see page 80)

375 g (12 oz) lean **pork**, sliced into thin strips

100 g (7 oz) **French beans**, topped and cut in half

2 tablespoons **Thai fish sauce (nam pla)**

1 teaspoon **caster sugar**

Chinese chives or **regular chives**, to garnish

Heat the oil in a wok over a medium heat until the oil starts to shimmer. Add the curry paste and cook, stirring, until it releases its aroma.

Add the pork and French beans and stir-fry for 2–3 minutes until the meat is cooked through and the beans are just tender.

Stir in the fish sauce and sugar and serve, garnished with Chinese chives or regular chives.

For chicken green curry with sugar snap peas,

cook as above, replacing the red curry paste with 1½ tablespoons green curry paste, the pork with 375 g (12 oz) sliced chicken breast and the French beans with 100 g (7 oz) sliced sugar snap peas. Add a dash of lime juice before serving.

pork with broccoli & mushrooms

Serves **4**

Preparation time **10 minutes**

Cooking time **10 minutes**

1 tablespoon **sesame seeds**

3 tablespoons **groundnut oil**

400 g (13 oz) lean **pork**, sliced into thin strips

250 g (8 oz) small **broccoli** florets

150 g (5 oz) **shiitake mushrooms**, trimmed and halved, if large

3 **baby leeks**, trimmed, cleaned and thinly sliced

3 tablespoons **Chinese rice wine** or **dry sherry**

3 tablespoons **oyster sauce**

2 tablespoons **malt vinegar**

1 teaspoon **caster sugar**

1 teaspoon **clear honey**

½ teaspoon **sesame oil**

1 **red chilli**, thinly sliced

Fry the sesame seeds in a dry wok over a medium heat, stirring until golden. Set aside.

Heat half the oil in a wok over a high heat until the oil starts to shimmer. Add half the pork and stir-fry for 2 minutes until golden. Remove the pork using a slotted spoon and set aside. Heat the remaining oil and stir-fry the rest of the pork in the same way, then return the first batch of pork to the wok.

Add the broccoli, mushrooms and leeks and stir-fry for 2 minutes. Add the rice wine, oyster sauce, malt vinegar, sugar and honey and cook for 1 more minute. Remove from the heat, stir in the toasted sesame seeds, sesame oil and chilli, and serve.

For spring onion rice, to serve with the pork, heat 1 tablespoon groundnut oil in a wok over a high heat. Add 4 sliced spring onions and give them a quick stir, then tip in 250 g (8 oz) cold cooked rice. Stir until heated through, then add ½ teaspoon sesame oil and 1 tablespoon light soy sauce. Stir well and serve.

chinese five-spice spareribs

Serves **4**

Preparation time **5 minutes**, plus marinating

Cooking time **50 minutes**

2 **garlic cloves**, finely chopped

2 teaspoons finely chopped **fresh root ginger**

2 tablespoons **Chinese rice wine** or **dry sherry**

3 tablespoons **light soy sauce**

½ teaspoon **salt**

½ teaspoon **Chinese five-spice powder**

1 tablespoon **demerara sugar**

1 kg (2 lb) **pork spareribs**, separated and cut into 7 cm (3 inch) lengths using a cleaver

2 tablespoons **groundnut oil**

100 ml (3½ fl oz) **water**

1 shredded **spring onion**, to garnish

Place the garlic, ginger, rice wine, soy sauce, salt, Chinese five-spice powder and sugar in a bowl and mix to form a paste. Add the ribs and toss them in the marinade with your hands until they are well coated. Cover and leave to marinate for 1 hour or up to overnight in the refrigerator.

Heat the groundnut oil in a wok over a high heat until the oil starts to shimmer. Add the ribs and stir-fry for 4–5 minutes until browned. Pour in the water, cover and simmer gently for 40–45 minutes, until deliciously golden and tender. Garnish with shredded spring onion.

For ribs with hoisin sauce & chilli, omit the Chinese five-spice powder from the marinade and instead add 3 tablespoons hoisin sauce and 1 teaspoon hot chilli powder. Marinate the ribs and cook as above.

poultry & eggs

cashew chicken with peppers

Serves **4**
Preparation time **10 minutes**
Cooking time **15 minutes**

2 tablespoons **groundnut oil**
625 g (1¼ lb) boneless,
   skinless **chicken breasts**,
   cut into 2.5cm (1 inch)
   pieces
50 g (2 oz) **cashew nuts**
2 **red peppers**, cored,
   deseeded and cut into large
   pieces
2 **garlic cloves**, chopped
6 **spring onions**, halved
   widthways and lengthways
salt

Sauce
1 tablespoon **Chinese rice**
   wine or **dry sherry**
1 teaspoon **sesame oil**
2 tablespoons **light soy**
   sauce
½ teaspoon **cornflour**
4 tablespoons **water**

Combine all the ingredients for the sauce and set the mixture aside.

Heat 1 tablespoon of the groundnut oil in a wok over a high heat until the oil starts to shimmer. Season the chicken with salt and tip half of it into the wok. Stir-fry for 2–3 minutes, until golden, then remove the chicken using a slotted spoon and set aside. Heat the remaining oil and stir-fry the rest of the chicken in the same way. Remove and set aside.

Add the cashews and red peppers to the wok and stir-fry for 1 minute. Add the garlic and spring onions and cook, stirring, for a further minute. Return the chicken to the wok and pour in the sauce. Cook for 3–4 minutes until the chicken is cooked through and the pepper is tender.

For cashew chicken with peppers & water chestnuts, add 8 halved water chestnuts to the wok with the peppers in the third step. After 1 minute add the garlic and the spring onions, cook for 1 minute, then return the chicken and add the sauce to the pan as described above. Stir in 75 g (3 oz) bean sprouts 1 minute before the end of cooking.

low-fat lemon chicken

Serves **4**
Preparation time **12 minutes**,
 plus marinating
Cooking time **8 minutes**

1 **egg**, lightly beaten
2 **garlic cloves**, sliced
2 small pieces of **lemon** rind,
 plus juice of **1** lemon
500 g (1 lb) boneless,
 skinless **chicken breasts**,
 cut into 5 mm (¼ inch) slices
2 tablespoons **cornflour**
1 tablespoon **rapeseed** or
 olive oil
1 **spring onion**, diagonally
 sliced into 1.5 cm (¾ inch)
 lengths
lemon slices, to garnish

Mix the egg, garlic and lemon rind together in a shallow dish, add the chicken and leave to marinate for 10–15 minutes.

Remove the lemon rind and add the cornflour to the marinated chicken. Mix thoroughly to distribute the cornflour evenly among the chicken slices.

Heat the oil in a wok over a high heat until the oil starts to shimmer. Add the chicken slices, making sure you leave a little space between them, and fry for 2 minutes on each side.

Reduce the heat to medium and stir-fry for 1 more minute or until the chicken is browned and cooked. Turn up the heat and pour in the lemon juice. Add the spring onion, garnish with lemon slices and serve immediately.

For warm lemon chicken & herb salad, cook the chicken as above then toss into a bowl with ½ sliced cucumber, a handful of coriander leaves, 6 torn basil leaves and 50 g (2 oz) wild rocket. Dress the salad lightly with ½ teaspoon sesame oil and 1 teaspoon rapeseed or olive oil.

chicken & aubergine curry

Serves **4**

Preparation time **25 minutes**

Cooking time **25 minutes**

3 tablespoons **vegetable oil**

2 tablespoons **ready-made** or **homemade Thai red curry paste** (see below)

300 g (10 oz) boneless, skinless **chicken breasts**, finely sliced

4 tablespoons **Thai fish sauce (nam pla)**

3 **kaffir lime leaves**

600 ml (1 pint) **water**

3 small **green aubergines**, quartered

125 g (4 oz) canned sliced **bamboo shoots**, drained

2 **green chillies**, deseeded and finely sliced, plus extra to garnish

handful of **Thai sweet basil leaves**, to garnish

Heat the oil in a wok over a moderate heat. Add the curry paste and stir-fry for 1 minute. Add the chicken, fish sauce and kaffir lime leaves, and stir-fry for 5 minutes.

Pour in the measurement water and bring to the boil, then lower the heat before adding the aubergines and bamboo shoots. Stir well and simmer for 10 minutes, stirring occasionally.

Stir the green chillies into the curry. Garnish with Thai sweet basil and green chilli slices and serve with rice, if liked.

For homemade Thai red curry paste, combine the following ingredients in a in a blender or food processor: 6 deseeded, soaked and roughly chopped dried red chillies, 2 tablespoons chopped lemon grass, 1 tablespoon each chopped shallots and chopped garlic, 1 teaspoon each chopped coriander root or stem, chopped galangal, cumin seeds, salt and shrimp paste, 2 teaspoons coriander seeds and 6 white peppercorns. Grind to a thick paste. Any paste not used in the recipe can be kept in an airtight container in the refrigerator for 3 weeks.

thai chicken & vegetable curry

Serves **4**

Preparation time **10 minutes**

Cooking time **20 minutes**

2 tablespoons **groundnut oil**

2 tablespoons **ready-made** or **homemade Thai green curry paste** (see page 112)

625 g (1¼ lb) boneless, skinless **chicken breasts**, cut into large chunks

400 ml (14 fl oz) **coconut milk**

1 tablespoon **demerara sugar**

2 **lemon grass stalks**, fat ends bashed with a rolling pin

2.5 cm (1 inch) piece **fresh root ginger**, thickly sliced

1½ tablespoons **Thai fish sauce (nam pla)**

rind of 1 **lime**

75 g (3 oz) **mangetout**, diagonally sliced

125 g (4 oz) **baby sweetcorn**, sliced in half lengthways

small handful of **coriander leaves**, plus a few extra whole leaves, to garnish

juice of 1 **lime**

Heat the oil in a wok over a moderate heat. Add the green curry paste and stir for about 1 minute. Stir in the chicken pieces and, when well coated in the paste, add the coconut milk, sugar, lemon grass and ginger. Stir in the fish sauce and lime rind and bring to the boil. Reduce the heat to a simmer and cook for 10 minutes until thickened slightly.

Add the mangetout and sweetcorn and simmer for a further 5 minutes, until tender. Remove from the heat. Remove the ginger and lemon grass from the curry and discard.

Stir in the coriander and lime juice. Let the curry cool slightly before serving garnished with a few whole coriander leaves. Serve with rice, if liked.

For vegetable green curry, follow the first stage of the recipe, omitting the chicken. Increase the mangetout to 200 g (7 oz) and also add at the same time 200 g (7 oz) trimmed and halved button mushrooms and 75 g (3 oz) peas. Simmer for 3 minutes, then stir in 125 g (4 oz) bean sprouts and cook for 2 minutes. Discard the ginger and lemon grass, then stir in the coriander and lime juice and garnish as above.

kung po chicken

Serves **4**
Preparation time **12 minutes**
Cooking time **7 minutes**

2 tablespoons **groundnut oil**
2–3 **red chillies**, deseeded
  and sliced
2 **garlic cloves**, finely
  chopped
400 g (13 oz) boneless,
  skinless **chicken breasts**,
  cut into 1 cm (½ inch) cubes
1 teaspoon **chilli bean sauce**
50 g (2 oz) canned sliced
  bamboo shoots, drained
50 g (2 oz) canned **water
  chestnuts**, drained
1 tablespoon **Chinese rice
  wine** or **dry sherry**
100 ml (3½ fl oz) **chicken
  stock** or **water**
1 teaspoon **cornflour** mixed to
  a paste with 1 tablespoon
  water
50 g (2 oz) **roasted unsalted
  peanuts**
2 **spring onions**, cut into
  1 cm (½ inch) lengths

Heat the oil in a wok over a high heat until the oil starts to shimmer. Add the chillies and garlic and stir-fry for a few seconds.

Add the chicken and chilli bean sauce and stir-fry for a couple of minutes, then add the bamboo shoots, water chestnuts, rice wine and stock and bring to the boil. Slowly add the cornflour paste, stirring until the sauce has thickened and turned transparent.

Stir the peanuts and spring onions into the dish just before serving.

For coconut rice, to serve with Kung Po Chicken, put 200 g (7 oz) washed Thai jasmine or long-grain rice in a saucepan and add 50 ml (2 fl oz) coconut milk. Pour in water to a level of 2.5 cm (1 inch) above the rice. Bring to the boil, then lower the heat to a slow simmer. Cover with a tightly fitting lid, cook for 10 minutes, then turn off the heat and let the rice steam in the pan for a further 10 minutes before serving.

chicken with leek & asparagus

Serves **4**

Preparation time **10 minutes**

Cooking time **12 minutes**

1 teaspoon **cornflour**

1 teaspoon **dark soy sauce**

2 tablespoons **water**

1 tablespoon **caster sugar**

1 tablespoon **malt vinegar**

3 tablespoons **groundnut oil**

625 g (1¼ lb) boneless,
  skinless **chicken breasts**,
  cut into thin strips

1 tablespoon chopped **fresh
  root ginger**

large pinch of **chilli flakes**

1 **leek**, thinly sliced

300 g (10 oz) **asparagus**,
  halved length- and
  widthways

salt and **white pepper**

Mix the cornflour and soy sauce to make a smooth paste, then add the water, sugar and malt vinegar. Set aside.

Heat half the oil in a wok over a high heat until the oil starts to shimmer. Add the chicken strips and season with salt and white pepper. Stir-fry for 3–4 minutes until golden, then remove the chicken with a slotted spoon and set aside.

Return the wok to the heat and pour in the remaining oil. Add the ginger, chilli and leek and stir-fry over a medium heat for 3–4 minutes, until the leeks have started to soften. Stir in the asparagus and cook for 1 minute.

Tip the chicken back into the wok and cook for 1 minute. Pour in the cornflour mixture and cook, stirring, until it becomes a thick and velvety sauce. Serve with rice, if liked.

For beef with leek & carrots, omit the chicken and cut 625 g (1¼ lb) beef into thin strips and stir-fry as above. Replace the asparagus with a large, thinly sliced carrot and stir-fry with the ginger, chilli and leeks, then add the beef and the cornflour mixture, as above.

chicken with burnt chilli paste

Serves **4**
Preparation time **7 minutes**
Cooking time **8 minutes**

3 tablespoons **groundnut or vegetable oil**
3–4 **dried red chillies**, finely chopped
2 **garlic cloves**, thinly sliced
375 g (12 oz) boneless, skinless **chicken breasts**, cubed
2 tablespoons **Thai fish sauce (nam pla)**
2 tablespoons **water**
2 teaspoons **sugar**
2 **red chillies**, sliced
10 **Thai basil leaves**, plus sprigs to garnish
4 **kaffir lime leaves**, shredded
125 g (4 oz) **roasted cashew nuts**

Burnt chilli paste
3 tablespoons **groundnut oil**
1 **red onion**, finely chopped
6–8 large **dried red chillies**, finely chopped
6 **garlic cloves**, finely chopped
2 tablespoons **fish sauce**
1 tablespoon **tamarind water**
2 tablespoons **soft brown sugar**

Make the burnt chilli paste first. Heat the oil, add the onion and fry until softened. Remove using a slotted spoon and set aside. Add the chillies and fry until blackened, then remove and set aside. Add the garlic and fry until golden brown, then remove.

Grind half the fried chillies coarsely in a pestle and mortar. Add the onion and garlic and blend to a coarse paste. Return the mixture to the oil remaining in the wok and add the fish sauce, tamarind water and sugar. Heat gently for 2–3 minutes, stirring constantly, then remove from the heat.

Heat the oil in a wok over a high heat until the oil starts to shimmer. Fry the dried chillies until blackened, then remove using a slotted spoon and set aside. Add the sliced garlic to the wok and stir-fry until beginning to brown.

Add the chicken and fry quickly on all sides. Crumble the fried chillies over the chicken and add the burnt chilli paste, fish sauce, measurement water, sugar and one of the sliced chillies to the pan. Stir-fry over a high heat.

Add the basil leaves, kaffir lime leaves and cashew nuts and stir-fry for a further 1 minute. Garnish with the remaining sliced red chilli and the basil sprigs.

For noodles with beef, asparagus & burnt chilli paste, replace the chicken with 300 g (10 oz) lean beef strips and 200 g (7 oz) asparagus spears, cut in half lengthways. Follow the recipe as above, then, when adding the herbs and cashews, toss in 150 g (5 oz) thin egg noodles, cooked to packet instructions.

cantonese lemon chicken

Serves **4**
Preparation time **5 minutes**,
  plus marinating
Cooking time **15 minutes**

1 **egg**
½ teaspoon **salt**
3 tablespoons **cornflour**
5 tablespoons **Chinese rice
  wine** or **dry sherry**
625 g (1¼ lb) boneless,
  skinless **chicken breasts**,
  cut into 5 cm (2 inch) pieces
groundnut oil, for deep-frying
100 ml (3½ fl oz) **chicken
  stock**
juice of 1 **lemon**
1 tablespoon **caster sugar**
2 **garlic cloves**, chopped
1 teaspoon **sesame oil**

To garnish
1 **lemon**, sliced
1 **spring onion**, cut into
  thin strips

Combine the egg, salt, 2 tablespoons of the cornflour and 2 tablespoons of the rice wine in a bowl. Toss in the chicken and leave to marinate for 30 minutes.

Pour enough oil into the wok to deep-fry the chicken, and heat it to 190°C (375°F), or until a cube of bread dropped into the oil turns golden in 20 seconds. Drain the chicken and carefully lower half of it into the oil. Deep-fry for 2 minutes, until golden and crisp, then remove using a slotted spoon and drain on kitchen paper. Fry the rest of the chicken in the same way.

Pour the chicken stock into a wok over a high heat. Stir in the lemon juice, sugar and garlic, and the remaining cornflour and rice wine. Bring to the boil, then stir in the fried chicken. Cook, stirring, for 1–2 minutes, until the meat is coated in a velvety glaze, then stir in the sesame oil and cook for 1 more minute. Garnish with the lemon slices and spring onion strips.

For chicken & sugar snap peas in a lemon sauce, omit the marinade. Season the chicken with salt and stir-fry it in 2 batches in groundnut oil for 3 minutes. Return all the chicken to the wok, tip in 150 g (5 oz) halved sugar snaps and stir-fry for 1 minute. Pour in the sauce and cook until it becomes thick and velvety.

cranberry chicken stir-fry

Serves **4**
Preparation time **20 minutes**
Cooking time **10 minutes**

2 tablespoons **vegetable oil**,
   plus extra for deep-frying
2 **shallots**, finely chopped
2.5 cm (1 inch) piece **fresh
   root ginger**, cut into
   matchsticks
2 **garlic cloves**, crushed
4 boneless, skinless **chicken
   breasts**, about 75 g (3 oz)
   each, thinly sliced
2 tablespoons **hoisin sauce**
2 tablespoons **oyster sauce**
1 tablespoon **light soy sauce**
25 g (1 oz) **dried cranberries**
4 **spring onions**, diagonally
   sliced
200 g (7 oz) **vegetables** such
   as bean sprouts, sliced
   green or red pepper or
   carrot strips
handful of **basil leaves**
1 large **red chilli**, deseeded
   and finely sliced

Heat the oil in a wok over a high heat until the oil
starts to shimmer. Stir-fry the shallots, ginger and garlic
for 30 seconds, then add the chicken and stir-fry for
2 minutes or until golden brown.

Add the hoisin, oyster and soy sauces and the dried
cranberries and stir-fry for a further 2 minutes. Check
that the chicken is cooked all the way through, then
add the spring onions and bean sprouts or other
vegetables and toss together for 3–4 minutes.

Heat 1 cm (½ inch) oil in a small saucepan and deep-
fry the basil leaves and red chilli in two batches for
10–30 seconds until crisp. Use the crispy basil leaves
and chilli as a topping for the stir-fry.

For light cranberry chicken stir-fry, omit the deep-
fried topping and replace the hoisin and oyster
sauces with 2 tablespoons chicken stock mixed with
2 tablespoons dark soy sauce and 2 tablespoons
Chinese rice wine or dry sherry. Stir in ¼ teaspoon
cornflour and add to the recipe in the second step
with the soy sauce and dried cranberries.

eggs with onion & oyster sauce

Serves **2**
Preparation time **5 minutes**
Cooking time **5 minutes**

4 large **eggs**
1 teaspoon chopped **fresh root ginger**
½ teaspoon **sesame oil**
4 tablespoons **groundnut oil**
1 tablespoon **oyster sauce**

To garnish
2 **spring onions**, sliced into thin rounds
1 **red chilli**, sliced into thin rings

Crack the eggs into a bowl and gently stir in the ginger and sesame oil, without breaking the yolks.

Heat half the groundnut oil in a wok over a high heat until the oil starts to shimmer. Pour in half the egg mixture and cook for 2 minutes, until the base of the eggs is crisp and golden.

Carefully drain off the oil and return the wok to the heat. Cook for 1 minute to really crisp up the eggs, then slide them on to plates while the yolks are still runny. Repeat with remaining egg mixture.

Drizzle with the oyster sauce and scatter over the spring onions and chilli to garnish.

For Chinese-style omelette, lightly stir 6 eggs with the ginger and sesame oil as described above. Season with salt and stir in 75 g (3 oz) bean sprouts and 2 sliced spring onions. Cook the eggs in the oil for 2 minutes as above, flip over with a spatula and cook for a further 2 minutes. Serve with a scattering of fresh coriander.

chicken with asparagus

Serves **4**
Preparation time **20 minutes**
Cooking time **15 minutes**

2 tablespoons **rapeseed** or
   olive oil
2 **garlic cloves**, crushed
2 tablespoons **lemon grass**,
   finely chopped
2 teaspoons finely chopped
   fresh root ginger
1 **onion**, sliced
500 g (1 lb) boneless, skinless
   chicken breasts, cut into
   strips
300 g (10 oz) **tomatoes**,
   chopped
350 g (12 oz) **asparagus**,
   halved length- and
   widthways
1 tablespoon **shoyu** or **tamari**
   sauce
½ teaspoon **black pepper**
handful of **Thai basil leaves**,
   to garnish

Heat the oil in a wok over a high heat until the oil starts to shimmer. Toss in the garlic, lemon grass, ginger and onion and stir-fry for about 5 minutes.

Add the chicken and stir-fry for 5–7 minutes until the chicken is browned and cooked.

Add the tomatoes, asparagus, shoyu or tamari sauce and black pepper and stir-fry for 2–3 minutes to warm through. Garnish with the Thai basil leaves.

For chicken with lemon grass, mushrooms & bean sprouts, replace the asparagus with 200 g (7 oz) trimmed button mushrooms and 75 g (3 oz) bean sprouts. Add them to the wok with the tomatoes, shoyu or tamari sauce and pepper.

smoked mustard chicken

Serves **4**
Preparation time **10 minutes**
Cooking time **20 minutes**

1 tablespoon **wholegrain
    mustard**
1 tablespoon **extra virgin
    olive oil**
4 **chicken breasts**, about
    175 g (6 oz) each
150 g (5 oz) uncooked **rice**
75 g (3 oz) **Earl Grey tea
    leaves**
salt and **black pepper**

For the salsa verde
handful of **flat leaf parsley**
handful of **mint leaves**
handful of **basil leaves**
1 teaspoon **capers**
2 **anchovies** in oil
1 **garlic clove**, crushed
4 tablespoons **olive oil**
1 tablespoon **red wine
    vinegar**

Stir together the mustard and olive oil and season with salt and pepper. Rub this mixture all over the chicken breasts and set aside.

Prepare the wok for smoking by lining it with foil, then add the rice and tea leaves, mixed together. Place a circular rack in the wok and place the wok over a high heat with the lid on. Heat until smoke starts to escape out of it.

Remove the lid and quickly sit the chicken on the rack. Replace the lid and cook for 3 minutes, then reduce the heat to medium and cook for a further 10 minutes. Turn the heat off and let the chicken sit in the wok for a further 5 minutes while you prepare the salsa verde.

Blend all the salsa verde ingredients in a mini food processor or chop them up finely by hand. Tip into a bowl and adjust the seasoning to taste. Serve the chicken warm or at room temperature with the salsa verde on the side and steamed vegetables such as tenderstem broccoli, if liked.

For fennel, lemon & honey smoked chicken, season 2 tablespoons clear honey with salt and pepper and smear all over 4 chicken breasts. Prepare the wok for smoking as above, using the contents of 10 fennel tea bags instead of the Earl Grey and adding the rind of 2 lemons to the mixture. Cook the chicken as above.

oriental duck with pineapple

Serves **4**

Preparation time **20 minutes**

Cooking time **1 hour 10 minutes**

2 kg (4 lb) oven-ready **duck**

1.2 litres (2 pints) **water**

3 tablespoons **dark soy sauce**

1 ripe **pineapple**

2 teaspoons **sesame oil**

2 **green chillies**, deseeded and thinly sliced

1 large **garlic clove**, crushed

250 g (8 oz) can **water chestnuts**, drained and sliced

1 bunch of **spring onions**, diagonally sliced

Cut the duck in half lengthways, using a meat cleaver and poultry scissors. Place the halves in a wok and pour in the measurement water, then add 1 tablespoon of the soy sauce. Put the lid on the wok and bring to the boil. Reduce the heat so that the liquid simmers steadily and cook for 1 hour.

Prepare the pineapple while the duck is cooking: trim the leaves off the top and cut off the stalk end. Cut off the peel and cut out all the spines, then slice the fruit in half lengthways and remove the hard core. Cut the pineapple halves into slices and set them aside.

Remove the duck from its stock using a slotted spoon or tongs and set aside. Pour the stock out of the wok and wipe out the wok. When the duck is cool enough to handle, cut all the meat off the bones and slice it into pieces.

Heat the sesame oil in the wok over a high heat until the oil starts to shimmer. Add the chillies, garlic and duck meat and stir-fry until lightly browned, then add the water chestnuts and pineapple and cook for 1–2 minutes. Stir in the remaining soy sauce and any juice from the fruit, and sprinkle with the spring onions. Cook for 1 minute and serve immediately.

For spiced duck with orange, halve the duck and place in a wok with 1 litre (1¾ pints) water, 200 ml (7 fl oz) dark soy sauce, 2 star anise, 1 cinnamon stick, 5 cloves and the pared rind of 1 orange. Complete the recipe as above, replacing the pineapple with 1 sliced orange.

thai duck jungle curry

Serves **4**
Preparation time **10 minutes**
Cooking time **8 minutes**

2 tablespoons **groundnut oil**
1½ tablespoons **ready-made**
or **homemade Thai red**
curry paste (see page 80)
200 g (7 oz) **duck breast**,
thinly sliced
1½ tablespoons **Thai fish**
sauce (nam pla)
200 ml (7 fl oz) **chicken stock**
½ teaspoon **demerara sugar**
75 g (3 oz) **Thai pea**
aubergines
50 g (2 oz) **green beans**, cut
into 2.5 cm (1 inch) lengths
4 **baby sweetcorn**, cut into
2.5 cm (1 inch) lengths
2.5 cm (1 inch) piece
galangal, shredded
3 **kaffir lime leaves**, torn
handful of **Thai basil**
2 tablespoons fresh **green**
peppercorns

Heat the oil in a wok over a high heat until the oil starts to shimmer. Add the curry paste and stir-fry for a few seconds until its aroma is released, then add the duck and fish sauce and stir-fry until well combined.

Pour in the stock and bring to the boil, then add the sugar, aubergines, beans, sweetcorn, galangal, lime leaves, basil and peppercorns. Simmer for 3–4 minutes, until the vegetables are just tender.

For coconut & beef curry with carrot & beans,
replace the duck with 200 g (7 oz) lean beef, cut into strips, and the stock with a 200 ml (7 fl oz) can coconut milk and cook as above. Add 200 g (7 oz) carrot matchsticks to the wok instead of the pea aubergines and baby sweetcorn.

stir-fried duck breast salad

Serves **4**
Preparation time **10 minutes**
Cooking time **10 minutes**

3 tablespoons **groundnut oil**
500 g (1 lb) boneless, skinless
  duck breasts, cut into thin
  slices
1 **carrot**
10 cm (4 inch) piece
  cucumber
150 g (5 oz) **iceberg lettuce**,
  finely shredded
1 **celery stick**, finely sliced
  diagonally
4 **spring onions**, finely sliced
  diagonally
handful of **mint leaves**, torn
salt and **black pepper**

Dressing
3 tablespoons **light olive oil**
2 tablespoons **malt vinegar**
2 tablespoons **light soy**
  sauce
2 teaspoons **light muscovado**
  sugar

Heat half the oil in a wok over a high heat until the oil starts to shimmer. Toss in half the duck, season with salt and pepper and stir-fry for 2 minutes, until browned yet still slightly pink in the centre. Remove the duck using a slotted spoon and wipe the wok clean with kitchen paper. Heat the remaining oil and stir-fry the rest of the duck in the same way.

Toss the cooked duck in a large bowl with the dressing ingredients. Leave to marinate while you prepare the rest of the salad.

Use a vegetable peeler to slice the carrot finely lengthways into paper-thin ribbons. Cut the cucumber in half lengthways and scoop out the seeds using a spoon. Place cut-side down on a chopping board and finely slice on the diagonal. Place the carrot and cucumber in a large bowl, then add the lettuce, celery, spring onions and mint.

Allow the duck to completely cool in the dressing, then toss it into the prepared salad.

For crunchy scallop salad, heat 2 tablespoons groundnut oil in a wok and stir-fry 12 scallops for 4 minutes, until golden but still slightly raw in the centre. Toss into the dressing and, once cooled, add to the remaining salad as above.

duck with hoisin sauce

Serves **4**

Preparation time **15 minutes**,
  plus marinating

Cooking time **8 minutes**

500 g (1 lb) **duck breasts**
  with skin, trimmed and cut
  into thin strips

2 **garlic cloves**, thinly sliced

3 tablespoons **hoisin sauce**

1½ tablespoons **malt vinegar**

1 tablespoon **Chinese rice
  wine** or **dry sherry**

1 tablespoon **light soy sauce**

1 teaspoon **caster sugar**

1 **red chilli**, deseeded and
  finely chopped

1 teaspoon **Chinese five-
  spice powder**

½ teaspoon **salt**

2 tablespoons **groundnut oil**

To garnish

5 cm (2 inch) piece **cucumber**,
  halved, deseeded and cut
  into strips

3 **spring onions**, cut into thin
  strips

Place the duck in bowl with the garlic, hoisin, vinegar, rice wine, soy sauce, sugar, chilli, Chinese five-spice powder and salt. Mix well to combine, then marinate, covered, in the refrigerator for 30 minutes.

Heat half the groundnut oil in a wok over a high heat until the oil starts to shimmer. Toss in half the duck with its marinade and stir-fry for 3 minutes, until cooked, yet still slightly pink in the centre. Use a slotted spoon to remove the duck from the pan, to drain away any excess fat and wipe the wok clean with kitchen paper. Heat the remaining oil and stir-fry the rest of the duck in the same way.

Serve the duck topped with a scattering of cucumber and spring onion strips.

For duck in hoisin sauce with vegetables, heat 1 tablespoon groundnut oil in a wok and use to stir-fry 250 g (8 oz) sliced broccoli florets and 250 g (8 oz) sliced carrots for 2–3 minutes. Remove the vegetables using a slotted spoon, then cook the marinated duck as above. Return all the duck and the vegetables to the wok and stir-fry for 1 minute. Serve with the spring onions, omitting the cucumber.

ginger & honey chicken

Serves **4**

Preparation time **15 minutes**, plus soaking

Cooking time **10–15 minutes**

2 tablespoons **vegetable oil**

3 boneless, skinless **chicken breasts**, chopped

3 **chicken livers**, chopped

1 **onion**, finely sliced

3 **garlic cloves**, crushed

2 tablespoons **dried black fungus** (cloud's ears), soaked in hot water for 20 minutes, then drained

2 tablespoons **light soy sauce**

1 tablespoon **honey**

50 g (2 oz) finely chopped **fresh root ginger**

5 **spring onions**, chopped

1 **red chilli**, deseeded and finely sliced into strips, to garnish

Heat the oil in a wok over a medium heat and add the chicken breasts and livers. Fry the chicken mixture for 5 minutes, then remove it using a slotted spoon and set aside.

Add the onion to the wok and fry it over a low heat until soft. Remove half the onions from the wok and set aside. Add the garlic and the drained mushrooms and stir-fry for 1 minute. Return the chicken mixture to the wok.

Stir together the soy sauce and honey in a bowl until blended, then pour this over the chicken and stir well. Add the ginger and stir-fry for 2–3 minutes. Finally, add the spring onions and garnish with the reserved onions and strips of red chilli. Serve immediately with medium rice noodles, if liked.

For ginger duck with honey, substitute 4 boneless duck breasts for the chicken and omit the chicken livers. Continue as in the main recipe, adding 1 head shredded pak choi or ½ head shredded Chinese leaves to the wok with the ginger.

108

stir-fried sesame chicken

Serves **4**

Preparation time **10 minutes**, plus marinating

Cooking time **10 minutes**

500 g (1 lb) boneless, skinless **chicken breasts**, cut into thin strips

juice of **1 lime**

½ tablespoon **sesame oil**

3 tablespoons **sesame seeds**

3 tablespoons **groundnut oil**

1 **red pepper**, deseeded and cut into strips

1 **yellow pepper**, deseeded and cut into strips

2 heads of **pak choi**, leaves separated

½ tablespoon **light soy sauce**

1 tablespoon **sweet chilli sauce**

salt

Marinate the chicken strips in the lime juice and sesame oil for 30 minutes, then pat dry with kitchen paper and season with salt. Place the sesame seeds on a plate and roll the chicken strips in them until they are coated.

Heat half the oil in a wok over a high heat until the oil starts to shimmer. Toss in the chicken strips and stir-fry for 2–3 minutes until golden, then tip on to a plate.

Return the wok to the heat and wipe it clean with kitchen paper. Add the remaining oil and, once it's hot, tip in the peppers and pak choi and stir-fry for 2 minutes. Stir in the soy and sweet chilli sauces and cook for 1 more minute, then return the chicken to the wok and stir-fry for 1–2 minutes until cooked through.

For sesame pork with easy satay sauce, bring 4 tablespoons each chunky peanut butter and coconut milk to the boil in a small pan with 1 deseeded and chopped red chilli and 1 tablespoon fish sauce. Simmer for 2–3 minutes until thickened. Coat 500 g (1 lb) lean pork strips in sesame seeds as above and stir-fry over a medium heat for 4–5 minutes. Serve with the cooled sauce.

thai green chicken curry

Serves **4**

Preparation time **25 minutes**

Cooking time **25 minutes**

2 tablespoons **groundnut oil**

2.5 cm (1 inch) piece finely
    chopped **fresh root ginger**

2 **shallots**, chopped

4 tablespoons **ready-made** or
    **homemade Thai green
    curry paste** (see below)

625 g (1¼ lb) boneless,
    skinless **chicken thighs**, cut
    into 5 cm (2 inch) pieces

300 ml (½ pint) canned
    coconut milk

4 tablespoons **Thai fish
    sauce (nam pla)**

1 teaspoon **soft brown sugar**

3 **kaffir lime leaves**, finely
    chopped

1 **green chilli**, deseeded and
    finely sliced

salt and **black pepper**

fried chopped **garlic**, to
    garnish

Heat the oil in a wok over a low heat. Add the ginger
and shallots and stir-fry for about 3 minutes or until
softened. Add the curry paste and fry for 2 minutes.

Add the chicken to the wok and stir until evenly coated
in the spice mixture. Fry for 3 minutes to seal the
chicken pieces, then stir in the coconut milk and bring
the curry to the boil. Reduce the heat and cook the
curry over a low heat, stirring occasionally, for about
10 minutes or until the chicken is cooked through
and the sauce has thickened.

Stir in the fish sauce, soft brown sugar, kaffir lime
leaves and chilli. Cook the curry for a further 5 minutes,
then add salt and pepper to taste. Garnish the curry
with fried garlic and serve with medium rice noodles,
if liked.

For homemade Thai green curry paste, put 15 small
green chillies, 4 halved garlic cloves, 2 finely chopped
lemon grass stalks, 2 kaffir lime leaves, 2 chopped
shallots, 50 g (2 oz) coriander leaves, stalks and
roots, 2.5 cm (1 inch) piece chopped fresh root
ginger, 2 teaspoons coriander seeds, 1 teaspoon
black peppercorns, 1 teaspoon finely grated lime
rind, ½ teaspoon salt and 2 tablespoons groundnut
oil into a blender or food processor and grind to a
thick paste. Any paste not used in the recipe can be
kept in an airtight container in the refrigerator for up
to 3 weeks.

crispy spiced chicken wings

Serves **4** as a starter
Preparation time **5 minutes**
Cooking time **18 minutes**

125 g (4 oz) **plain flour**
1 tablespoon **hot chilli powder**
½ teaspoon **salt**
12 **chicken wings**
vegetable oil, for deep-frying
1 **red chilli**, sliced into thin rounds
3 **spring onions**, thinly sliced
1 tablespoon finely chopped **fresh root ginger**
lime wedges, to serve

Place the flour, chilli powder and salt in a large bowl and combine thoroughly. Add the chicken wings and toss well to coat in the flour.

Pour enough oil into the wok to deep-fry the chicken, and heat it to 190°C (375°F), or until a cube of bread dropped into the oil turns golden in 20 seconds. Deep-fry 6 chicken wings for 6–7 minutes, turning them in the oil until golden and crisp, then remove using a slotted spoon and drain on kitchen paper. Fry the remaining chicken wings in the same way.

Lower the chilli, spring onions and ginger into the oil, using a slotted spoon, and sizzle until crisp and the chilli is a vibrant red. Drain thoroughly on kitchen paper.

Pile the chicken wings on to a serving plate. Scatter with the crispy chilli, spring onions and ginger and serve with the lime wedges.

For sweet chilli dip, to serve with the chicken wings, cut 3 slices from a cucumber and finely chop. Stir into a bowl with 1 tablespoon chopped coriander, the grated rind of 1 lime and 1 teaspoon Thai fish sauce (nam pla). Stir in 5 tablespoons sweet chilli sauce.

bamboo chicken with cashews

Serves **4**

Preparation time **10 minutes**

Cooking time **15 minutes**

250 ml (8 fl oz) **chicken stock**

400 g (13 oz) boneless, skinless **chicken breasts**, cubed

2 tablespoons **yellow bean sauce**

200 g (7 oz) **carrots**, sliced

200 g (7 oz) canned sliced **bamboo shoots**, drained

1 teaspoon **cornflour** mixed to a paste with 2 tablespoons **water**

125 g (4 oz) **cashew nuts**, toasted

1 **spring onion**, shredded

Heat the chicken stock in a wok. Add the chicken meat and bring the stock back to the boil, stirring, then lower the heat and cook for 5 minutes. Remove the chicken using a slotted spoon and set aside.

Add the yellow bean sauce to the wok and cook for 2 minutes. Add the carrots and bamboo shoots and cook for another 2 minutes.

Return the chicken to the pan, bring the sauce back to the boil and thicken with the cornflour paste. Stir in the cashews and spring onion just before serving.

For mild chicken curry with peanuts, cook the chicken as above. Replace the yellow bean sauce with ½ tablespoon mild Madras paste and cook for 2 minutes, then add the carrot with 200 g (7 oz) broccoli florets instead of the bamboo shoots. Continue the recipe as above, finishing by stirring in 125 g (4 oz) chopped roasted peanuts in place of the cashews and 2 sliced spring onions.

chicken livers with green beans

Serves **4** as a starter
Preparation time **15 minutes**
Cooking time **8 minutes**

500 g (1 lb) **chicken livers**
5 tablespoons **groundnut oil**
3 **shallots**, very thinly sliced
½ teaspoon finely sliced **fresh
  root ginger**
2 **garlic cloves**, finely sliced
1 **green chilli**, very thinly
  sliced
75 g (3 oz) **green beans**, cut
  into 1 cm (½ inch) slices
½ teaspoon **caster sugar**
1 tablespoon **malt vinegar**
1 tablespoon **Chinese rice
  wine** or **dry sherry**
2 tablespoons **oyster sauce**
2 handfuls of shredded
  iceberg lettuce
salt and **black pepper**
dried chilli flakes, to serve

Trim away any white membrane of the chicken livers
and pat the livers dry with kitchen paper. Lightly season
with salt and pepper and set aside.

Heat the oil in a wok over a high heat until the oil
starts to shimmer. Tip in the shallots and give them a
quick stir, then add the ginger, garlic and chilli. Fry until
crisp but not too dark, then remove using a slotted
spoon and drain on kitchen paper.

Toss in half the chicken livers and cook over a high
heat for 1 minute on each side until just browned.
Set aside and fry the remaining livers in the same
way, adding some more oil to the wok if needed.

Return all the livers to the wok, then toss in the
beans and stir-fry for 1 minute. Stir in the remaining
ingredients and continue cooking until the livers are
well coated in a rich sauce.

Spoon on to a serving dish with the shredded lettuce
and spoon the crispy shallot mixture over the top. Serve
with a small bowl of dried chilli flakes on the side.

For warm chicken liver salad, cook the livers
as above, then toss into a bowl with 75 g (3 oz)
watercress, approximately 10 cucumber slices
and 1 tablespoon toasted sesame seeds. Serve
as a starter or light lunch.

chinese five-spice citrus quail

Serves **4** as a starter
Preparation time **10 minutes**
Cooking time **15 minutes**

4 x 125 g (4 oz) **quails**
1 tablespoon **Chinese five-spice powder**
½ teaspoon **salt**
2 tablespoons **cornflour**
4 tablespoons **plain flour**
vegetable oil, for deep-frying
2 **garlic cloves**, chopped
1 teaspoon finely chopped **fresh root ginger**
3 tablespoons **dark soy sauce**
3 tablespoons **orange juice**
2 tablespoons **Chinese rice wine** or **dry sherry**
4 tablespoons **water**
1 tablespoon **soft brown sugar**
juice of 1 **lime**

To garnish
3 **spring onions**, chopped
rind of 1 **orange**
lime wedges

Cut each quail into quarters, using a cleaver or kitchen shears, then dry well on kitchen paper. Combine the Chinese five-spice powder, salt, cornflour and plain flour in a large bowl, then toss in the quail quarters.

Pour enough oil into the wok to deep-fry the quail, and heat it to 190°C (375°F), or until a cube of bread dropped into the oil turns golden in 20 seconds. Deep-fry half the quail pieces for 4–5 minutes, until golden and crisp, then remove using a slotted spoon and drain on kitchen paper. Fry the remaining quail pieces in the same way and set aside.

Drain away all but 1 tablespoon of the oil. Return the wok to the heat and add the garlic and ginger, stirring well. Pour in the soy sauce, orange juice, rice wine and water. Stir in the sugar and, once it has dissolved, toss in the fried quail pieces. Cook, stirring, until the pieces are well coated in a velvety sauce, then remove from the heat and toss in the lime juice. Serve with a scattering of spring onions and the orange rind, with lime wedges on the side.

For orange, fennel & radish salad, to serve as an accompaniment, use a vegetable peeler to cut 1 small fennel bulb into paper-thin slices. Toss in a bowl with 1 orange, divided into segments, 4 finely sliced radishes, ¼ teaspoon sesame oil, 1 teaspoon light olive oil and a pinch of salt. Squeeze in a dash of lime juice and use as a bed for the quail.

fish &
shellfish

steamed citrus sea bass

Serves **4**
Preparation time **15 minutes**
Cooking time **20 minutes**

1 whole **sea bream** or **sea
  bass**, about 800–900 g
  (1 lb 10 oz–2 lb), scaled
  and gutted
50 ml (2 fl oz) **chicken stock**
  or **water**
50 ml (2 fl oz) **Chinese rice
  wine** or **dry sherry**
rind of 1 small **orange**, thinly
  sliced
2.5 cm (1 inch) piece **fresh
  root ginger**, thinly sliced
1 teaspoon **caster sugar**
3 tablespoons **light soy
  sauce**
½ teaspoon **sesame oil**
1 **garlic clove**, thinly sliced
3 **spring onions**, thinly sliced
1 tablespoon **groundnut oil**

Score 3 diagonal slits along each side of the fish with
a sharp knife, then cut in the opposite direction to
make a diamond pattern.

Cut 2 large pieces of foil about 1½ times the length of
the fish. Place the fish in the centre of the double layer
of foil and lift it up around the fish slightly. Pour the
stock and rice wine over the fish, then scatter with
the orange rind and half the ginger.

Place a circular rack inside a wok and pour in enough
water to come just below the top of the rack. Place
the lid on the wok and bring the water to a rolling boil.
Carefully sit the open fish parcel on the rack, cover
with the lid and steam for 15–18 minutes until the
flesh inside the slits is opaque. Carefully remove the
fish from the wok and place on a serving dish.

Stir the sugar into a bowl with the soy sauce and
sesame oil, then pour the liquid over the fish with
the garlic, spring onions and remaining ginger.

Heat the groundnut oil in a small frying pan over a high
heat until smoking hot, then pour it over the fish. This
will crisp up the spring onions and ginger and release
their aroma. Serve immediately.

**For steamed sea bream with mushrooms &
tomatoes**, place the fish on the foil as above and
season with salt and pepper. Top with 2 tablespoons
olive oil, 100 ml (3½ fl oz) dry white wine, 75 g (3 oz)
trimmed and sliced shiitake mushrooms and 6 halved
cherry tomatoes. Steam in the wok as above.

scallops with lemon & ginger

Serves **3–4**
Preparation time **10 minutes**
Cooking time **10 minutes**

15 g (½ oz) **butter**
2 tablespoons **vegetable oil**
8 **scallops**, cut into thick
slices
½ bunch of **spring onions**,
thinly sliced diagonally
½ teaspoon **ground turmeric**
3 tablespoons **lemon juice**
2 tablespoons **Chinese rice
wine** or **dry sherry**
2 pieces **preserved stem
ginger** with syrup, chopped
salt and **pepper**

Heat a wok until hot. Add the butter and 1 tablespoon of the oil and heat over a gentle heat until foaming. Add the sliced scallops and stir-fry for 3 minutes, then remove using a slotted spoon and set aside on a plate.

Return the wok to a moderate heat, add the remaining oil and heat until the oil starts to shimmer. Add the spring onions and turmeric and stir-fry for a few seconds. Add the lemon juice and rice wine and bring to a boil, then stir in the stem ginger.

Return the scallops and their juices to the wok and toss until heated through. Season with salt and pepper to taste and serve immediately.

For fennel & carrot salad, to serve with the scallops, use a vegetable peeler to cut 1 fennel bulb and 2 carrots into thin shavings. Toss into a bowl with a handful of coriander leaves, the juice of ½ lemon and ½ teaspoon sesame oil.

sweet & sour monkfish & prawns

Serves **4**
Preparation time **10 minutes**
Cooking time **7 minutes**

300 g (10 oz) **monkfish tail**,
  cut into chunks
200 g (7 oz) raw peeled **tiger
  prawns**
2 tablespoons **groundnut oil**
1 tablespoon chopped **fresh
  root ginger**
200 g (7 oz) **carrots**, cut into
  matchsticks
200 g (7 oz) **sugar snap
  peas**, halved
4 **spring onions**, thinly sliced
salt and **black pepper**

Sweet and sour sauce
150 ml (5 fl oz) **fish** or
  vegetable stock
2½ tablespoons **light soy
  sauce**
2 teaspoons **tomato purée**
1 tablespoon **cider vinegar**
2 teaspoons **caster sugar**
2 teaspoons **cornflour**
½ teaspoon **salt**

Combine all the ingredients for the sauce. Season the monkfish and prawns with salt and pepper.

Heat the oil in a wok over a high heat until the oil starts to shimmer. Add the fish and prawns and cook for 2 minutes, carefully turning the fish occasionally, then tip in the ginger, carrots, sugar snaps and spring onions.

Fry for 30 seconds, then add the sauce and bring to the boil. Turn down the heat and simmer for 2–3 minutes until the vegetables are just tender and the fish is cooked through. Serve immediately.

For aromatic monkfish & prawns, cook the fish as above up to the stage where you would have added the sweet and sour sauce. Omit this and instead stir-fry for a further 2 minutes, then remove from the heat and toss in a handful each of torn coriander and mint and the juice of 1 lime.

seafood & vegetable stir-fry

Serves **4**

Preparation time **18 minutes**

Cooking time **10 minutes**

250 g (8 oz) **live mussels**

250 g (8 oz) **water chestnuts,** peeled and thickly sliced

1 tablespoon **caster sugar**

½ teaspoon **black pepper**

2 tablespoons **vegetable oil**

1 **sweet white onion**, sliced

125 g (4 oz) raw peeled **tiger prawns**

4 **spring onions,** trimmed and diagonally sliced

½ teaspoon **crushed chilli flakes,** plus extra to garnish

125 g (4 oz) **sugar snap peas**, trimmed and diagonally halved

125 g (4 oz) **bean sprouts**

3 tablespoons **light soy sauce**

2 tablespoons **yellow bean sauce**

2 tablespoons **Chinese rice wine** or **dry sherry**

chervil sprigs, to garnish

Scrub the mussels thoroughly under cold running water. Pull off the hairy 'beards' and rinse again. Gently tap any open mussels and discard any that do not close.

Sprinkle the water chestnuts with the sugar and pepper and set aside.

Heat the oil in a wok over a high heat until the oil starts to shimmer. Add the onion and mussels and stir-fry quickly for 1 minute. Put a lid on the wok and cook for 3–4 minutes or until the mussels have opened. Discard any mussels that remain closed.

Add the water chestnuts, prawns, spring onions, chilli flakes, sugar snaps and bean sprouts to the wok and stir-fry for 1–2 minutes or until the prawns have turned pink and are cooked through.

Mix together the soy sauce, yellow bean sauce and rice wine and pour over the ingredients in the wok. Stir-fry for a further 1–2 minutes until hot. Garnish with crushed chilli flakes and chervil sprigs. Serve with rice, if liked.

For quick mixed seafood stir-fry, replace the live mussels and raw prawns with 250 g (8 oz) mixed cooked seafood, now available in most supermarkets. Cook the onions as above, then add the mixed seafood to the wok at the same time as the sauce ingredients. Complete the recipe as above.

thai basil & chilli clams

Serves **4** as a starter
Preparation time **10 minutes**,
  plus soaking
Cooking time **6 minutes**

500 g (1 lb) small **clams**
2 tablespoons **groundnut oil**
2 **garlic cloves**, finely
  chopped
1 tablespoon chopped **fresh
  root ginger**
2 tablespoons **Thai fish
  sauce (nam pla)**
1 tablespoon **chilli oil**
½ teaspoon **demerara sugar**
2 **red chillies**, 1 cut into rings,
  and 1 sliced and deseeded,
  to garnish
handful of **Thai basil leaves**

Wash the clams under cold running water, discarding
any that are broken or that remain open when tapped.
Soak them in plenty of cold water for 30 minutes, then
drain and rinse again in cold running water. Place in a
bowl, cover with a wet tea towel and keep refrigerated
until needed.

Heat the oil in a wok over a high heat until the oil
starts to shimmer. Add the garlic and ginger and stir-fry
for a few seconds. Add the clams and all the remaining
ingredients, reserving the 1 sliced chilli to garnish.
Cook, stirring, for 4–5 minutes until the clams open.
Serve immediately, discarding any clams that remain
closed. Garnish with slices of red chilli.

For seafood noodles, stir-fry 500 g (1 lb) raw
peeled king prawns in 1 tablespoon groundnut oil
for 2 minutes. Add 300 g (10 oz) squid rings and fry
for 1 more minute, then remove using a slotted spoon
and follow the recipe as above. Once the clams are
cooked, return the prawns and squid to the pan, add
300 g (10 oz) cooked thick dried rice noodles and stir
until steaming hot. Serve with lime wedges.

seafood with cellophane noodles

Serves **4–6**
Preparation time **5 minutes**
Cooking time **20 minutes**

1 tablespoon **rapeseed** or
olive oil
2 **garlic cloves**, chopped
1 tablespoon chopped **fresh
root ginger**
1 tablespoon **chilli bean
sauce**
2 teaspoons **shoyu** or **tamari
sauce**
1 teaspoon **white pepper**
2 litres (3½ pints) **fish** or
vegetable stock
225 g (7½ oz) **Chinese
leaves**, cut into 2.5 cm
(1 inch) strips
175 g (6 oz) **dried
cellophane noodles**
125 g (4 oz) raw peeled **tiger
prawns**
125 g (4 oz) **scallops**
125 g (4 oz) cleaned **squid**,
cut into 1cm (½ inch) rings
1 tablespoon **coriander
leaves**, to garnish

Heat the oil in a wok over a high heat until the oil
starts to shimmer. Add the garlic and ginger and stir-fry
for a few seconds until fragrant.

Stir in the chilli bean sauce, shoyu sauce, pepper and
stock and bring to the boil. Add the Chinese leaves,
turn down the heat to medium and simmer for
10 minutes.

Add the cellophane noodles, cover the wok and
simmer for another 5 minutes, then add the prawns,
scallops and squid, stir and bring back to the boil.
Simmer for 1 more minute, then serve in a deep
dish and garnish with coriander leaves.

For warm seafood & cellophane noodle salad, soak
the noodles according to the packet instructions, then
refresh in cold running water and drain. Cook the
garlic and ginger as above, then add the chilli bean
sauce, shoyu, pepper and 2 tablespoons stock or
water. Omit the Chinese leaves and add the seafood.
Stir-fry for 3 minutes, then toss into the cooked
noodles with a good handful each of coriander
and mint leaves.

salt & pepper squid

Serves **4** as a starter
Preparation time **10 minutes**
Cooking time **6 minutes**

1 teaspoon **Szechuan peppercorns**
1 teaspoon **sea salt**
1½ tablespoons **cornflour**
1½ tablespoons **plain flour**
1 teaspoon **hot chilli powder**
625 g (1¼ lb) cleaned **squid**, cut into 1cm (½ inch) rings
vegetable oil, for deep-frying
1 **red chilli**, thinly sliced
3 **spring onions**, sliced
coriander leaves, to garnish

Place the Szechuan peppercorns in a dry wok and stir over a medium heat until they begin to pop and release their aroma. Transfer to a pestle and mortar and pound with the salt until coarsely ground.

Place the salt and pepper mixture, flours and chilli powder in a bowl and toss in the squid rings.

Pour enough oil for deep-frying the squid into a wok, and heat it to 190°C (375°F), or until a cube of bread dropped into the oil turns golden in 20 seconds. Add half the squid and deep-fry for about 1 minute until lightly coloured, then remove using a slotted spoon and drain on kitchen paper. Fry the remaining squid in the same way.

Place the chilli and spring onions in a slotted spoon and gently lower the spoon into the hot oil for a few seconds. Serve the squid with a scattering of coriander and the crispy chilli and spring onions.

For cucumber, bean sprout & watercress salad,

to serve as an accompaniment, peel ½ cucumber and cut it in half lengthways. Scoop out the seeds and slice thinly. Toss into a bowl with 50 g (2 oz) bean sprouts, 50 g (2 oz) watercress, 1 tablespoon light soy sauce, 1 teaspoon sesame oil and 1 pinch each sugar and salt.

scallops in a rich szechuan sauce

Serves **4**
Preparation time **10 minutes**
Cooking time **5 minutes**

2 tablespoons **groundnut oil**
1 tablespoon finely chopped **fresh root ginger**
2 **garlic cloves**, crushed
3 **spring onions**, cut into thin strips
12 **scallops**
150 g (5 oz) **carrots**, cut into sticks
1 **celery stick**, sliced
1 teaspoon **sesame oil**
handful of **coriander leaves**, to garnish

Szechuan sauce
1 tablespoon **light soy sauce**
1 tablespoon **tomato purée**
1 tablespoon **Chinese rice wine** or **dry sherry**
1 tablespoon **chilli sauce**
½ teaspoon **salt**
¼ teaspoon **black pepper**

Combine all the ingredients for the sauce and set aside.

Heat the oil in a wok over a high heat until the oil starts to shimmer. Add the ginger, garlic and spring onions and stir-fry for a few seconds before adding the scallops. Stir-fry for 1 minute until they begin to colour, add the carrots and celery, then pour in the sauce.

Cook for a further 2 minutes, until the vegetables are just tender and everything is coated in a rich glaze. Add the sesame oil and cook for a further 30 seconds. Remove from the heat and serve garnished with a scattering of coriander leaves.

For pork spareribs with Szechuan sauce, make the Szechuan sauce as described above and omit the rest of the ingredients apart from the groundnut oil. Separate 1 kg (2 lb) pork spareribs and cut into 7 cm (3 inch) lengths using a clever. Marinate the ribs in the sauce for 1 hour or up to overnight. Heat the oil in a wok over a high heat, add the ribs and stir-fry for 4–5 minutes until browned. Pour in 100 ml (3¾ fl oz) water, cover and simmer gently for 40–45 minutes until tender. Garnish with 1 shredded spring onion.

squid stir-fried with mangetout

Serves **2**
Preparation time **12 minutes**
Cooking time **8 minutes**

250 g (8 oz) cleaned **squid**
1 tablespoon **rapeseed** or
   olive oil
1 **green chilli**, deseeded and
   chopped
2 teaspoons **Szechuan**
   peppercorns, crushed
2 **garlic cloves**, crushed
1 small **onion**, chopped
250 g (8 oz) **mangetout**
2 teaspoons **shoyu** or **tamari**
   sauce
1 tablespoon **Chinese rice**
   wine or **dry sherry**

Cut the squid into slices and use a sharp knife to score with a criss-cross pattern. (This makes them curl up when they are cooked and the grooves help to trap the sauce.)

Heat the oil in a wok over a high heat until the oil starts to shimmer. Reduce the heat to medium, add the chilli, peppercorns, garlic and onion and stir-fry for 3–4 minutes.

Turn the heat to high, add the squid slices and stir-fry quickly for 1 minute, then remove using a slotted spoon and set aside.

Toss in the mangetout and stir-fry for 1 minute, then return the squid to the wok and stir to mix. Add the shoyu sauce and rice wine and stir-fry for a few seconds, then serve immediately.

For squid with peas & chilli tomato, prepare and stir-fry the squid for 1 minute as above. Add 125 g (4 oz) fresh or frozen peas and stir-fry for another 30 seconds. Stir in ½ tablespoon tomato purée mixed with the Chinese rice wine, shoyu sauce and ½ red chilli cut into thin rings. Stir for a final 30 seconds and serve.

tea-smoked salmon

Serves **4**
Preparation time **10 minutes**,
   plus marinating
Cooking time **15 minutes**

4 x skinless **salmon fillets**,
   about 125 g (4 oz) each
125 g (4 oz) **demerara sugar**
3 tablespoons **sea salt**
2 tablespoons **extra virgin**
   olive oil
150 g (5 oz) uncooked **rice**
50 g (2 oz) **green tea leaves**
1 **lemon**, cut into wedges,
   to serve

Sauce
juice of ½ **lemon**
1 tablespoon chopped
   parsley
4 tablespoons **mayonnaise**
salt and **black pepper**

Lay the salmon on a plate and rub it all over with the sugar, salt and olive oil. Cover and chill in the refrigerator for 1 hour, then wipe all the marinade off the salmon and discard.

Prepare the wok for smoking by lining it with foil, then mix in the rice and tea leaves. Place a circular rack in the wok and place the wok over a high heat with the lid on. Heat until smoke starts to escape out of it.

Remove the lid and quickly sit the salmon on the rack. Replace the lid and cook for 2 minutes, then reduce the heat to medium and cook for a further 4 minutes. Turn the heat off and let the salmon sit in the wok for a further 6 minutes while you prepare the sauce.

Stir the lemon juice and parsley into the mayonnaise and season with freshly ground black pepper. Serve the salmon with the lemon wedges and the flavoured mayonnaise in a small bowl, and accompany with some salad leaves, if liked.

For tea-smoked salmon salad, smoke the salmon as above, then flake into a bowl with 150 g (5 oz) blanched French beans, 125 g (4 oz) halved cherry tomatoes and 20 g (¾ oz) flat leaf parsley leaves. Season with salt and pepper, then gently toss in 2 tablespoons extra virgin olive oil and a generous squeeze of lemon.

monkfish stir-fried with celery

Serves **4**
Preparation time **10 minutes**
Cooking time **7 minutes**

1 tablespoon **rapeseed** or
  olive oil
1½ tablespoons chopped
  fresh root ginger
500 g (1 lb) **monkfish fillets**,
  cut into 1 cm (½ inch) slices
100 ml (3½ fl oz) hot **fish
  stock**
1 teaspoon **shoyu** or **tamari
  sauce**
1 tablespoon **Chinese rice
  wine** or **dry sherry**
1 teaspoon **white pepper**
½ teaspoon **sesame oil**
500 g (1 lb) tender **celery
  hearts**, cut into 2.5 x 1 cm
  (1 x ½ inch) pieces
2 teaspoons **cornflour** mixed
  to a paste with 2 tablespoons
  water or **stock**

Heat the oil in a wok over a high heat until the oil
starts to shimmer. Add the ginger and stir-fry for a
few seconds until fragrant.

Add the monkfish and stir-fry for 1 minute, then add
the hot stock and bring to the boil. Add the shoyu
sauce, rice wine, pepper and sesame oil and stir.

Add the celery and bring the mixture back to boil,
then add the cornflour paste, stirring until the sauce
has thickened and has turned translucent.

For beef with celery & tomatoes, replace the
monkfish with 500 g (1 lb) lean beef, cut into 1 cm
(½ inch) thick slices. Use 100 ml (3 ½ oz) hot chicken
stock instead of the fish. Add 4 quartered tomatoes to
the wok with the celery and finish the recipe as above.

mussels in black bean sauce

Serves **4** as a starter
Preparation time **15 minutes**
Cooking time **7 minutes**

1 kg (2 lb) **live mussels**
1 tablespoon **groundnut oil**
2 **garlic cloves**, finely sliced
2 tablespoons **black bean
  sauce**
1 tablespoon chopped **fresh
  root ginger**
2 tablespoons **Chinese rice
  wine** or **dry sherry**
1 tablespoon **light soy sauce**
4 tablespoons **water**
handful of **coriander leaves**,
  roughly chopped

Scrub the mussels thoroughly under cold running water. Pull off the hairy 'beards' and rinse again. Gently tap any open mussels and discard any that don't close.

Heat the oil in a wok over a medium heat. Add the garlic and fry until crisp and golden. Now stir in the black bean sauce, ginger, rice wine and soy sauce. Pour in the water and boil for 1 minute.

Throw in the mussels, cover and simmer over a medium heat for 3–4 minutes, until all the mussels have opened, discarding any that remain closed. Stir in the coriander and serve immediately.

For king prawns with oyster sauce, heat the oil and add all the ingredients for the sauce, replacing the black bean sauce with oyster sauce. Omit the mussels and add 250 g (8 oz) raw peeled king prawns. Simmer for 2–3 minutes until pink all the way through and serve with a scattering of shredded spring onions.

thai yellow prawn curry

Serves **4**

Preparation time **10 minutes**

Cooking time **15 minutes**

3 tablespoons **groundnut oil**

1 recipe quantity **ready-made
or homemade Thai yellow
curry paste** (see below)

125 ml (4 fl oz) **water**

250 ml (8 fl oz) canned
coconut milk

20 raw peeled **king prawns**

2 teaspoons **Thai fish sauce
(nam pla)**

1 teaspoon **lime juice**

salt and **black pepper**

To garnish

2 **red chillies**, deseeded and
finely sliced

1 tablespoon chopped
coriander

Heat the oil in a wok over a low heat. Add the curry
paste and stir-fry for 4 minutes, until the paste is
fragrant. Stir the measurement water into the curry
paste, bring to the boil and cook over a high heat for
2 minutes to reduce the paste.

Stir the coconut milk into the curry paste, then add the
prawns. Cook the curry over a medium heat, stirring
occasionally, for about 6 minutes or until the prawns
turn pink and are cooked through.

Stir in the fish sauce and lime juice, and season to
taste with salt and pepper. Transfer to a warm serving
plate. Garnish with the sliced chillies and coriander, and
serve with rice, if liked.

For homemade Thai yellow curry paste, put finely
chopped 2.5 cm (1 inch) galangal, 1 finely chopped
lemon grass stalk, 2 chopped shallots, 3 chopped
garlic cloves, 2 teaspoons ground turmeric,
1 teaspoon each ground coriander, ground cumin
and shrimp paste and ½ teaspoon chilli powder in a
blender or food processor and grind to a thick paste.

prawns & scallops with asparagus

Serves **4**
Preparation time **5 minutes**
Cooking time **10 minutes**

12 raw peeled **king prawns**
8 **scallops**
3 tablespoons **groundnut oil**
2.5 cm (1 inch) piece **fresh root ginger**, finely chopped
2 **garlic cloves**, crushed
250 g (8 oz) **asparagus**, cut into 2.5 (1 inch) lengths
2 tablespoons **Chinese rice wine** or **dry sherry**
1 tablespoon **malt vinegar**
1½ tablespoons **light soy sauce**
2 teaspoons **caster sugar**
100 ml (3½ fl oz) **water**
½ teaspoon **sesame oil**
salt and **white pepper**

Season the prawns and scallops with salt and freshly ground white pepper.

Heat 1 tablespoon of the oil in a wok over a high heat until the oil starts to shimmer. Add the prawns and stir-fry for 2 minutes until they begin to colour, then remove using a slotted spoon and set aside. Add another tablespoon of the oil to the wok and, once it is hot, stir-fry the scallops for 1 minute on each side. Remove using a slotted spoon and set aside.

Heat the remaining oil in the wok. Stir in the ginger, garlic and asparagus and stir-fry for 1 minute, then add the rice wine, vinegar, soy sauce, sugar and water and bring to the boil. Return the prawns and scallops to the wok and stir-fry until they are cooked and the asparagus is just tender. Add the sesame oil and give everything a good stir, then serve.

For king prawns with peppers & sesame seeds,
use 16 raw peeled king prawns instead of the scallops. Replace the asparagus with 1 red and 1 yellow pepper, cored, deseeded and cut into thin strips. Cook as above, finishing with 2 tablespoons toasted sesame seeds.

aromatic thai crab

Serves **4** as a starter
Preparation time **20 minutes**
Cooking time **5 minutes**

2 cooked whole **crabs**,
  each weighing about
  750 g (1½ lb)
3 tablespoons **groundnut oil**
1 **red chilli**, cut into thin
  rounds
2 **lemon grass stalks**, finely
  sliced
3 **garlic cloves**, thinly sliced
6 x 1 cm (½ inch) slices **fresh
  root ginger**
2 tablespoons **light soy
  sauce**
2 tablespoons **Thai fish
  sauce (nam pla)**
2 tablespoons **sweet chilli
  sauce**
2 tablespoons **water**
juice of 1 **lime**
handful of **mint leaves**
handful of **coriander leaves**

Prepare the crab by by hitting the back underside of the shell, which loosens the meat. With the shell towards you, stand the crab up and force the body away from the shell using your thumbs. Pull off the tail and discard it, then twist off the claws and smash them open by hitting them with a rolling pin. Pull away the gills that lie along the body and discard them. Using a sharp knife, split the body into quarters.

Heat the oil in a wok over a high heat until the oil starts to shimmer. Add the chilli, lemon grass, garlic and ginger and stir-fry for 30 seconds. Pour in the soy, fish and sweet chilli sauces and water.

Add the crab and stir-fry for 2–3 minutes until well coated in the sauce and warmed through, then remove from the heat. Stir in the lime juice and fresh herbs.

For aromatic crab noodles, use 200 g (7 oz) cooked crabmeat instead of the whole crab. Cook with the other ingredients as above, adding 200 g (7 oz) soaked thick dried rice noodles and 150 g (5 oz) halved cherry tomatoes to the wok with the crab.

fish with black bean sauce

Serves **4**
Preparation time **15 minutes**
Cooking time **25–30 minutes**

1 tablespoon **sesame oil**
25 g (1 oz) **fresh root ginger**, cut into fine strips
1 large **garlic clove**, chopped
3 tablespoons **salted black beans**
1 tablespoon **lemon juice**
2 tablespoons **light soy sauce**
2 teaspoons **caster sugar**
150 ml (¼ pint) **Chinese rice wine** or **dry sherry**
750 g (1½ lb) thick **white fish fillet** (for example cod, haddock or coley), skinned and cut into 2 pieces
4 large **spring onions**, finely sliced diagonally, plus extra to garnish
1 **red pepper**, cored, deseeded, grilled and cut into fine strips, to garnish

Heat the oil in a wok over a moderate heat. Add the ginger and garlic with the black beans and stir-fry for 2 minutes, then stir in the lemon juice, soy sauce, sugar and rice wine.

Lay the fish fillets in the sauce in the wok. Simmer gently for 20–25 minutes, by which time the fish should be cooked through. Sprinkle the spring onions over the top of the fish and cook for just a few minutes longer.

Transfer the fish and sauce to a warm serving dish or, alternatively, divide into 4 portions and serve on individual plates. Garnish with the red pepper strips and spring onions and serve immediately with rice noodles, if liked.

For chicken with black bean sauce, substitute 750 g (1½ lb) thinly sliced boneless, skinless chicken for the fish. Add to the sauce and simmer for 15–20 minutes, or until cooked through. Continue as in the main recipe and serve hot.

crunchy thai seafood salad

Serves **4**
Preparation time **15 minutes**
Cooking time **5 minutes**

125 g (4 oz) **bean sprouts**
4 **spring onions**, thinly sliced
75 g (3 oz) **sugar snap peas**,
  thinly sliced
5 cm (2 inch) piece **cucumber**,
  peeled and thinly sliced
125 g (4 oz) **cherry
  tomatoes**, halved
handful of **mint leaves**
handful of **coriander leaves**
2 tablespoons **groundnut oil**
1 **garlic clove**, chopped
1 tablespoon finely chopped
  fresh root ginger
325 g (11 oz) cleaned **squid**,
  cut into 1 cm (½ inch) rings
8 **fish balls**
8 raw peeled **king prawns**
1 **red chilli**, deseeded and
  finely chopped
1 teaspoon **demerara sugar**
2 tablespoons **Thai fish
  sauce (nam pla)**
2 **kaffir lime leaves**, shredded
juice of 1 **lime**
½ tablespoon **sesame oil**
1 tablespoon **light soy sauce**
sweet chilli sauce, to serve

Combine the bean sprouts, spring onions, sugar snaps, cucumber and tomatoes in a large serving dish, then toss in the herbs.

Heat the oil in a wok over a high heat until the oil starts to shimmer. Add the garlic and ginger and stir-fry for 30 seconds, then add the squid, fish balls and prawns and stir-fry for 2–3 minutes until just cooked.

Add the chilli, sugar, fish sauce and lime leaves. Continue stir-frying for 1 minute, then toss into the salad bowl with the lime juice, sesame oil and soy sauce. Serve with sweet chilli sauce on the side.

For chicken salad with coconut, prepare the salad as above, replacing the seafood with 625 g (1¼ lb) chicken breast cut into strips. Once ready, toss 50 g (2 oz) fresh coconut shards into the salad.

mild thai fish curry

Serves **4**
Preparation time **10 minutes**
Cooking time **25 minutes**

5 tablespoons **groundnut oil**
6 **Thai shallots**, thinly sliced
1 tablespoon **ready-made or homemade Thai red curry paste** (see page 80)
4 **kaffir lime leaves**, torn
2 tablespoons **Thai fish sauce (nam pla)**
½ tablespoon **demerara sugar**
400 ml (14 fl oz) **coconut milk**
500 ml (17 fl oz) **vegetable stock**
6 **baby aubergines**, quartered
125 g (4 oz) **mangetout**, halved
750 g (1½ lb) skinned **cod** or **haddock**, cut into 3.5 cm (1 ½ inch) pieces
150 g (5 oz) **cherry tomatoes**, halved
handful of **Thai basil leaves**

Heat the oil in a wok over a high heat until the oil starts to shimmer. Add the shallots and fry until golden and crisp, then remove using a slotted spoon and drain on kitchen paper.

Drain all but 2 tablespoons of the oil from the pan and use to stir-fry the curry paste for 30 seconds. Stir in lime leaves, fish sauce, sugar, coconut milk and vegetable stock and bring to the boil. Lower the heat and simmer very gently for 10 minutes.

Stir in the aubergine and cook for a further 5 minutes, then gently fold in the mangetout and fish and cook for 2 minutes. Add the tomatoes and half the Thai basil leaves. Cook for a final 2 minutes, then top with the crisp shallots and the remaining basil leaves.

For spicy mixed seafood curry, use 3 tablespoons ready-made or homemade Thai red curry paste (see page 80). Reduce the quantity of white fish to 250 g (8 oz). When adding it to the coconut broth, also fold in 150 g (5 oz) small raw prawns and 200 g (7 oz) squid rings and continue as above.

cabbage, prawn & pork salad

Serves **4**
Preparation time **15 minutes**
Cooking time **10 minutes**

300 g (10 oz) **white cabbage**,
  finely sliced
12 peeled cooked **king
  prawns**
125 g (4 oz) sliced **roast pork**
3 tablespoons **vegetable oil**
3 **shallots**, finely sliced
2 tablespoons roughly
  chopped **roasted peanuts**

Dressing
1 **garlic clove**, crushed
1 tablespoon **Thai fish sauce
  (nam pla)**
juice of 2 **limes**
1 teaspoon **sesame oil**
1 tablespoon **light soy sauce**
1 tablespoon **groundnut oil**

Combine all the ingredients for the salad dressing and
set aside.

Cook the cabbage in boiling water for 2 minutes,
then drain and refresh under cold running water.
Drain thoroughly, then toss the cabbage in a bowl
with the dressing.

Add the prawns and pork to the cabbage and stir well
to combine, then set aside while you fry the shallots.

Heat the oil in a wok over a high heat. When the oil
starts to shimmer, add the shallots and stir-fry until
crisp and golden. Remove from the wok using a slotted
spoon and drain thoroughly. Scatter the crispy shallots
and the chopped peanuts over the salad, then serve.

For courgette, prawn & pork salad, omit the cabbage
and instead slice 1 large courgette and stir-fry in a
wok in 1 tablespoon vegetable oil until just tender.
Combine the cooked courgettes with the prepared
salad dressing, the prawns and the pork, then fry
the shallots as above. Replace the peanuts with
1 tablespoon roughly chopped roasted cashews.

seafood with fresh peppercorns

Serves **4**

Preparation time **5 minutes**

Cooking time **5 minutes**

3 tablespoons **groundnut oil**

2 **garlic cloves**, finely chopped

4 **scallops**, quartered

6 **crab sticks**, halved in length

200 g (7 oz) peeled cooked **king prawns**

1 tablespoon **Thai fish sauce (nam pla)**

1 tablespoon **oyster sauce**

1 tablespoon **light soy sauce**

1 teaspoon **demerara sugar**

2 tablespoons **fresh green peppercorns**

Heat the oil in a wok over a high heat until the oil starts to shimmer. Add the garlic and stir-fry for a few seconds, then tip in the scallops and stir-fry for 1 minute until golden.

Add the crab sticks, prawns, fish, oyster and soy sauces, sugar and peppercorns, in that order, giving the dish a quick stir between each addition.

Cook for 1 more minute, until all the fish is heated through and well coated in the sauce. Serve with rice, if liked.

For coconut rice with seafood & fresh peppercorns,

cook the dish as above, remove from the heat and set aside. Heat 1 tablespoon groundnut oil in a wok and pour in 5 tablespoons coconut milk. Bring to the boil with 1 teaspoon fish sauce, stir in 250 g (8 oz) cooked jasmine rice and heat through, then add the cooked seafood. Cook for 30 seconds and serve with a squeeze of lime juice.

chilli prawns with garlic & spinach

Serves **4**
Preparation time **10 minutes**
Cooking time **5 minutes**

2 tablespoons **vegetable oil**
1 **garlic clove**, sliced
1 **red birds eye chilli**,
  deseeded and chopped
300 g (10 oz) **baby spinach**
125 g (4 oz) raw peeled **tiger
  prawns**
3 tablespoons **light soy
  sauce**
2 teaspoons **caster sugar**
1 tablespoon **Chinese rice
  wine** or **dry sherry**
1 tablespoon **Thai fish sauce
  (nam pla)**
6 tablespoons **water**
Chinese chive flowers or
  chives, to garnish

Heat the oil in a wok over a high heat until the oil
starts to shimmer. Add the garlic and chilli and stir-fry
for 30 seconds.

Add the spinach and prawns and stir-fry in the oil for
1–2 minutes until the spinach begins to wilt and the
prawns are pink and cooked through.

Mix the soy sauce, sugar, rice wine, fish sauce and
water together and add to the pan. Quickly stir-fry
together for another minute and serve while the
spinach still has texture. Garnish with Chinese
chive flowers or chives.

For monkfish with lime & spinach, replace the
prawns with 250 g (8 oz) monkfish cut into large
chunks. Stir-fry the fish with the garlic, chilli and
spinach as above, adding in the grated rind and
juice of 1 lime with the soy sauce as you remove
the stir-fry from the heat.

vegetables
& tofu

thai yellow vegetable curry

Serves **4**

Preparation time **15 minutes**

Cooking time **30 minutes**

1 tablespoon **groundnut oil**

1 **onion**, sliced

400 ml (14 fl oz) **coconut milk**

200 ml (7 fl oz) **light vegetable stock**

2 tablespoons **ready-made** or **homemade Thai yellow curry paste** (see page 148)

1 tablespoon **demerara sugar**

3 tablespoons **Thai fish sauce (nam pla)**

750 g (1½ lb) **new potatoes**, peeled and quartered

250 g (8 oz) **carrots**, sliced

250 g (8 oz) **cauliflower florets**

75 g (3 oz) **fresh** or **frozen peas**

handful of **coriander leaves**, to garnish

Heat the oil in a wok over a moderate heat. Add the onion and stir-fry for 4–5 minutes, until they are slightly golden. Remove using a slotted spoon and set aside.

Pour the coconut milk and stock into the wok and increase the heat to bring the liquid quickly to the boil. Add the curry paste, sugar and fish sauce and mix until combined.

Add the potatoes, carrots and fried onion, lower the heat and simmer for 10 minutes. Add the cauliflower and peas and cook for a further 10 minutes, by which time all the vegetables should be tender.

Tip into a large serving bowl and top with a scattering of coriander.

For Thai yellow chicken & vegetable curry, omit the carrots and cauliflower. Cut 625 g (1¼ lb) boned and skinned chicken thighs into quarters and add these to the wok with the potatoes. Simmer for 10 minutes. Add the peas, then complete the recipe as above.

stir-fried asparagus & mushrooms

Serves **4**
Preparation time **5 minutes**
Cooking time **7 minutes**

1½ tablespoons **groundnut oil**
375 g (12 oz) **asparagus**,
  trimmed and sliced in half
  diagonally
1 **red onion**, cut into wedges
2 **garlic cloves**, finely
  chopped
125 g (4 oz) **oyster**
  mushrooms, trimmed and
  torn, if large
2 tablespoons **Chinese rice**
  wine or **dry sherry**
2 tablespoons **vegetable**
  stock or **water**
1 tablespoon **oyster sauce**
1 tablespoon **malt vinegar**
2 teaspoon **caster sugar**
1 teaspoon **salt**
1 teaspoon **sesame oil**

Heat the oil in a wok over a high heat until the oil starts to shimmer. Add the asparagus and onion and stir-fry for 2 minutes, then add the garlic and mushrooms and cook, stirring, for another minute.

Combine the rice wine, stock, oyster sauce, vinegar, sugar, salt and sesame oil and pour the mixture into the wok. Stir-fry for 1–2 minutes until the vegetables are well coated in a velvety sauce, then serve.

For rice with duck & asparagus, slice 275 g (9 oz) duck breast and stir-fry in 2 tablespoons groundnut oil until just golden. Omit the mushrooms and add the asparagus, onion and garlic to the pan. Cook for 2 minutes, then add the sauce ingredients combined as in the second step, together with 250 g (8 oz) cooked jasmine rice. Stir-fry until the jasmine rice is heated through.

thai red tofu & vegetable curry

Serves **4**
Preparation time **15 minutes**
Cooking time **25–30 minutes**

450 g (14½ oz) **firm tofu**
1 tablespoon **rapeseed** or **olive oil**
2 tablespoons **ready-made** or **homemade Thai red curry paste** (see page 80)
1–2 **green chillies**, sliced
200 ml (7 fl oz) canned **light coconut milk**
250 ml (8 fl oz) **vegetable stock**
1 large **aubergine**, diced
12 **baby sweetcorn**
100 g (3½ oz) **mangetout**
100 g (3½ oz) **carrots**, sliced
125 g (4 oz) **shiitake mushrooms**, halved
1 large **green pepper**, sliced
150 g (5 oz) canned sliced **bamboo shoots**, drained
1 tablespoon **Thai fish sauce (nam pla)**
1 tablespoon **clear honey**
2 **kaffir lime leaves**

To garnish
large handful of torn **Thai basil leaves**
handful of toasted **cashew nuts**

Drain the tofu and pat it dry with kitchen paper before cutting it into 5 cm (2 inch) cubes.

Heat the oil in a wok over high heat until the oil starts to shimmer. Stir-fry the red curry paste and chillies for 1 minute, then stir in 2 tablespoons of the coconut milk (from the thicker part at the top of the can) and cook, stirring constantly, for 2 minutes.

Add the stock and bring to the boil. Add the aubergine, then bring the mixture back to the boil and simmer for about 5 minutes. Add the remaining vegetables and cook for another 5–10 minutes. Stir in the fish sauce, honey, lime leaves and the remaining coconut milk and simmer for another 5 minutes, stirring occasionally. Add the tofu cubes and mix well.

Garnish with torn Thai basil leaves and toasted cashew nuts. Serve with jasmine or sticky (glutinous) rice, if liked, which will absorb all the wonderful aromatic sauce.

For one-pot tofu & vegetable noodles, use 400 ml (14 fl oz) coconut milk and increase the quantity of stock to 350 ml (12 fl oz). Add 200 g (7 oz) cooked thick rice noodles along with the tofu and simmer for 1 minute before serving with the garnish above.

pak choi with chilli & ginger

Serves **4**
Preparation time **5 minutes**
Cooking time **5 minutes**

1 tablespoon **groundnut oil**
½ **chilli**, sliced into rings
1 tablespoon chopped **fresh root ginger**
large pinch of **salt**
500 g (1 lb) **pak choi**, leaves separated
100 ml (3½ fl oz) **water**
¼ teaspoon **sesame oil**

Heat the oil in a wok over a high heat until the oil starts to shimmer. Add the chilli, ginger and salt and stir-fry for 15 seconds.

Tip the pak choi into the wok and stir-fry for 1 minute, then add the water and continue stirring until the pak choi is tender and the water has evaporated. Toss in the sesame oil and serve immediately.

For pak choi & shiiitake mushrooms with chilli, ginger & oyster sauce, cook as above, adding 250 g (8 oz) trimmed and sliced shiitake mushrooms with the pak choi and stirring 2 tablespoons oyster sauce into the wok together with the water.

spicy tempeh & vegetable stir-fry

Serves **4**
Preparation time **12 minutes**
Cooking time **10 minutes**

1 tablespoon **rapeseed or olive oil**

2 **red chillies**, sliced

2 **lemon grass stalks**, finely sliced

2 **kaffir lime leaves**

1 large **garlic clove**, crushed

1 tablespoon chopped **fresh root ginger**

1 tablespoon **tamarind paste**

2 tablespoons **vegetable stock**

2 teaspoons **shoyu** or **tamari sauce**

1 tablespoon **clear honey**

500 g (1 lb) **tempeh** or **firm tofu**, cut into strips

125 g (4 oz) **baby sweetcorn**

125 g (4 oz) **asparagus**, halved

Heat the oil in a wok over a high heat until the oil starts to shimmer. Add the chillies, lemon grass, lime leaves, garlic and ginger, then turn the heat down to medium and stir-fry for 2–3 minutes.

Add the tamarind paste, stock, shoyu sauce and honey and cook for 2–3 minutes until the sauce has become thick and glossy.

Add the tempeh, sweetcorn and asparagus and stir-fry for about 2 minutes to warm through, then serve.

For prawns with lemon grass & tamarind paste, replace the tempeh or tofu with 500 g (1 lb) raw peeled king prawns and cook as above. Omit the sweetcorn and stir in a handful of coriander leaves just before removing the wok from the heat.

garlicky choi sum

Serves **4**

Preparation time **5 minutes**

Cooking time **5 minutes**

500 g (1 lb) **choi sum**

2 tablespoons **groundnut oil**

3 **garlic cloves**, sliced

1 tablespoon **salt**

2 tablespoons **Chinese rice wine** or **dry sherry**

150 ml (¼ pint) **water**

1 teaspoon **sesame oil**

Trim 5 cm (2 inches) from the ends of the choi sum, then cut it into 5 cm (2 inch) lengths. Wash thoroughly.

Heat the oil in a wok over a high heat until the oil starts to shimmer. Add the garlic and salt and stir-fry for 15 seconds, then tip in the choi sum and stir-fry for 1 minute.

Add the rice wine and water and stir-fry for 2–3 minutes, until the choi sum is tender and most of the liquid has evaporated. Stir in the sesame oil and serve immediately.

For pak choi with water chestnuts & garlic, follow the recipe as above, replacing the choi sum with 500 g (1 lb) pak choi, cut into 5 cm (2 inch) lengths, and 4 halved tinned water chestnuts.

mixed vegetable chop suey

Serves **4**
Preparation time **10 minutes**
Cooking time **8 minutes**

1 tablespoon **cornflour**
1 tablespoon **light soy sauce**
1 tablespoon **Chinese rice
 wine** or **dry sherry**
3 tablespoons **vegetable
 stock** or **water**
½ teaspoon **clear honey**
2 tablespoons **groundnut oil**
2 **red peppers**, cored,
 deseeded and cut into strips
2 **shallots**, finely sliced
1 teaspoon chopped **fresh
 root ginger**
2 **garlic cloves**, chopped
150 g (5 oz) **shiitake
 mushrooms**, trimmed and
 halved
50 g (2 oz) canned sliced
 bamboo shoots, drained
50 g (2 oz) drained canned
 water chestnuts
300 g (10 oz) **bean sprouts**
3 **spring onions**, cut into
 2.5 cm (1 inch) lengths

Put the cornflour into a cup with the soy sauce and
rice wine and stir to a smooth paste. Add the stock
and honey and set the sauce aside.

Heat the oil in a wok over a high heat until the oil
starts to shimmer. Add the red peppers, shallots, ginger
and garlic and stir-fry for 2 minutes, then add the
mushrooms, bamboo shoots and water chestnuts
and stir-fry for 2 more minutes.

Add the bean sprouts to the pan with the spring
onions and the prepared sauce. Continue cooking
for 1–2 minutes, or until the vegetables are coated
in a rich velvety glaze. Serve immediately.

For beef chop suey with Chinese leaves, stir-fry
300 g (10 oz) lean beef strips in 2 tablespoons
groundnut oil for 2–3 minutes until browned, then
remove using a slotted spoon. Follow the recipe
above, omitting the bamboo shoots and reducing
the bean sprouts to 150 g (5 oz). When adding
the mushrooms, also stir in 200 g (7 oz) shredded
Chinese leaves. Return the beef to the wok when
adding the sauce.

vegetables with sweet chilli sauce

Serves **4**

Preparation time **10 minutes**

Cooking time **5 minutes**

250 g (8 oz) **chestnut mushrooms**, trimmed and halved

2 tablespoons **cornflour**

2 tablespoons **groundnut oil**

1 tablespoon chopped **fresh root ginger**

2 **garlic cloves,** thinly sliced

½ teaspoon **salt**

2 **red peppers,** cored, deseeded and cut into chunks

4 small heads **pak choi,** cut in half lengthways

2 tablespoons **Chinese rice wine** or **dry sherry**

1 tablespoon **dark soy sauce**

1 tablespoon **sweet chilli sauce**

4 **spring onions,** thinly sliced

Place the mushrooms in a bowl with the cornflour and toss to coat. Set aside.

Heat the oil in a wok over a high heat until the oil starts to shimmer. Add the ginger, garlic and salt and stir quickly, then add the mushrooms, red peppers and pak choi and stir-fry for 2–3 minutes until just tender.

Stir in the rice wine, soy and sweet chilli sauces and spring onions and cook for 1 more minute, until the sauce has thickened.

For spiced rice & mixed vegetables with oyster sauce, cook the vegetables as described above, omitting the salt. Stir in 4 tablespoons oyster sauce and 300 g (10 oz) cooked Thai jasmine rice with the rice wine, soy sauce and spring onions. Replace the sweet chilli sauce with 2 teaspoons Chinese chilli oil.

aromatic carrot & mixed nut salad

Serves **6**
Preparation time **10 minutes**
Cooking time **10 minutes**

2 teaspoons **groundnut oil**
3 tablespoons **cashew nuts**
3 tablespoons **peanuts**
¼ teaspoon **salt**
1 **green chilli**, deseeded and
    finely chopped
1 teaspoon chopped **fresh
    root ginger**
500 g (1 lb) **carrots**, coarsely
    grated
3 **shallots,** finely sliced
grated rind and juice of **1 lime**
½ teaspoon **sesame oil**
handful of torn **mint leaves**
handful of **coriander leaves**

Heat the oil in a wok over a moderate heat. Add the nuts and stir-fry for 3–4 minutes, or until golden.

Add the salt, chilli and ginger and stir-fry for 30 seconds, then toss into a bowl with the carrots, shallots, lime rind and juice, sesame oil and herbs. Set aside until the nuts have cooled and serve as a refreshing side dish.

For seared tuna & mixed nut salad, cook the nuts with the salt, chilli and ginger as above, then toss in a handful of coriander leaves and 75 g (3 oz) wild rocket. Dress with the lime and sesame oil. Pan-fry or griddle a thick 250 g (8 oz) tuna steak for 1 minute on each side, then slice and gently fold into the rocket and nuts.

malaysian spicy cauliflower

Serves **4**
Preparation time **10 minutes**
Cooking time **10 minutes**

2 tablespoons **groundnut oil**
1 **red chilli**, deseeded and
    finely chopped
1 **onion**, thickly sliced
2 **garlic cloves,** chopped
1 teaspoon **dried shrimp
    paste**
1 teaspoon **salt**
500g (1 lb) **cauliflower**, cut
    into florets then sliced
3 tablespoons **water**

Heat the oil in a wok over a high heat until the oil
starts to shimmer. Add the chilli, onion and garlic
and stir-fry for 1 minute.

Add the shrimp paste, using the back of a spoon to
break it up. Stir-fry for 1 minute then tip in the salt
and cauliflower. Stir well to combine all the flavours
then sprinkle with the water, cover and steam for
3–4 minutes, until tender.

For spicy cauliflower soup, start the recipe as above,
adding 250 g (8 oz) peeled and diced floury potatoes
with the cauliflower. Once all the flavours are tossed
together, pour in 1 litre (1¾ pints) vegetable stock.
Simmer for 15 minutes, then blend until smooth.
Serve with a drizzle of chilli oil.

vegetables in yellow bean sauce

Serves **4**

Preparation time **5 minutes**

Cooking time **6–7 minutes**

2 tablespoons **groundnut oil**

1 teaspoon chopped **fresh root ginger**

2 **garlic cloves**, thinly sliced

½ teaspoon **salt**

200 g (7 oz) canned sliced **bamboo shoots**, drained

300 g (10 oz) **broccoli florets**

2 tablespoons **yellow bean sauce**

3 tablespoons **Chinese rice wine** or **dry sherry**

4 tablespoons **water**

Heat the oil in a wok over a high heat until the oil starts to shimmer. Stir in the ginger, garlic and salt and stir-fry for 30 seconds, then add the bamboo shoots and broccoli and stir-fry for 2 minutes.

Stir in the yellow bean sauce and cook for 1 minute, then add the rice wine and water. Continue stir-frying until the vegetables are coated in a rich velvety sauce. Serve immediately with rice, if liked.

For broccoli stir-fried rice, follow the recipe as above, omitting the bamboo shoots and the yellow bean sauce. Once the recipe is completed, stir in 250 g (8 oz) cooked jasmine rice and stir-fry until warmed through. Remove from the heat and stir in ¼ teaspoon sesame oil.

chinese leaves in spicy sauce

Serves **4**
Preparation time **5 minutes**
Cooking time **4 minutes**

2 tablespoons **groundnut oil**
6 x 1 cm (½ inch) slices **fresh root ginger**
2 **garlic cloves**, thinly sliced
1 teaspoon **salt**
300 g (10 oz) **Chinese leaves**, cut into 3.5 cm (1½ inch) pieces
3 tablespoons **Chinese rice wine** or **dry sherry**
1 tablespoon **oyster sauce**
1 tablespoon **malt vinegar**
2 teaspoons **caster sugar**
½ teaspoon **sesame oil**

Heat the oil in a wok over a high heat until the oil starts to shimmer. Add the ginger, garlic and salt and stir-fry for 30 seconds.

Tip in the Chinese leaves and stir for 30 seconds, then add the rice wine, oyster sauce, vinegar, sugar and oil and stir-fry for a further 2 minutes until just tender.

For spicy prawns & Chinese leaves with nuts,

fry 1 sliced red chilli and 200 g (7 oz) raw peeled prawns with the ginger, garlic and salt. Add the Chinese leaves and other ingredients, then finish the completed dish by scattering with 2 tablespoons crushed toasted cashews.

tofu with mushrooms

Serves **4**
Preparation time **10 minutes**
Cooking time **10 minutes**

450 g (14½ oz) **firm tofu**
vegetable oil, for deep-frying
1 teaspoon finely chopped
   fresh root ginger
2 **garlic cloves**, finely
   chopped
200 g (7 oz) **shiitake**
   mushrooms, trimmed and
   halved, if large
125 g (4 oz) **sugar snap**
   peas, halved
2 tablespoons **oyster sauce**
2 tablespoons **Chinese rice**
   wine or **dry sherry**
1 **red chilli**, finely sliced and
   deseeded, to garnish

Drain the tofu and pat dry with kitchen paper before cutting it into 20 equal-sized cubes. Set aside. Pour enough oil for deep-frying the tofu into a wok, and heat it to 190°C (375°F), or until a cube of bread dropped into the oil turns golden in 20 seconds. Add half the tofu and deep-fry until puffy and golden, then remove using a slotted spoon and drain on kitchen paper. Sir-fry the remaining tofu in the same way. Set aside.

Pour off all but 2 tablespoons of the oil and place the wok over a high heat. Add the ginger and garlic and give it a quick stir, then add the mushrooms and sugar snaps.

Stir-fry for 2 minutes, then return the tofu to the pan and toss in the oyster sauce and rice wine. Cook, stirring, for a further 1–2 minutes until the tofu is well coated and has soaked up some of the sauce. Remove from the heat and serve with a scattering of sliced chilli.

For prawns with shiitake mushrooms & peas, omit the tofu, fry the garlic and ginger as above, then add 250 g (8 oz) raw peeled prawns, 200 g (7 oz) sliced shiitake mushrooms and 125 g (4 oz) fresh or defrosted peas, instead of the sugar snaps. Complete the recipe as above.

chilli kale

Serves **4**
Preparation time **8 minutes**
Cooking time **17 minutes**

1 tablespoon **olive oil**
1 **garlic clove**, crushed
1 large **white onion**, chopped
500 g (1 lb) **curly kale**, stalks
    removed and leaves
    chopped
2 teaspoons **lime juice**
1 **red chilli**, deseeded and
    chopped
1 teaspoon **salt**
½ teaspoon **black pepper**

Heat the oil in a wok over a moderate heat. Add the garlic and onion and sauté for about 10 minutes or until the onion is translucent. Add the curly kale and stir-fry for another 5 minutes.

Stir in the lime juice and chilli, season with salt and pepper to taste and serve immediately.

For chilli cabbage, replace the curly kale with 500 g (1 lb) cabbage. Discard the stalks and tough outer leaves, then chop the leaves before frying with the garlic and onion and finishing as above. This dish also works well with spring greens.

tofu & vegetables in oyster sauce

Serves **4**

Preparation time **10 minutes**

Cooking time **12 minutes**

450 g (14½ oz) **firm tofu**

200 ml (7 fl oz) **vegetable oil**

1 teaspoon chopped **fresh root ginger**

2 **garlic cloves**, finely chopped

5 **spring onions**, cut into 2.5 cm (1 inch) lengths

50 g (2 oz) tinned **water chestnuts**, halved

75g (3 oz) **mangetout**, cut in half on the diagonal

½ **red onion**, cut into thin wedges

1 teaspoon **sesame oil**

Oyster sauce

1½ tablespoons **Chinese rice wine** or **dry sherry**

3 tablespoons **chicken stock** or **water**

1 tablespoon **oyster sauce**

2 teaspoons **light soy sauce**

2 teaspoons **caster sugar**

2 teaspoons **malt vinegar**

½ teaspoons **salt**

Combine the ingredients for the oyster sauce and set aside.

Drain the tofu and pat it dry with kitchen paper before cutting it into 20 equal-sized cubes. Pour enough oil into the wok to deep-fry the tofu, and heat it to 190°C (375°F), or until a cube of bread dropped into the oil turns golden in 20 seconds. Add half the tofu and deep-fry until puffy and golden, then remove using a slotted spoon and drain on kitchen paper. Fry the rest of the tofu in the same way. Set aside.

Pour off all but 2 tablespoons of the oil and place the wok over a high heat. Add the ginger, garlic and spring onions and give them a quick stir, then add the water chestnuts, mangetout and red onion. Stir-fry for 2 minutes, until softened slightly, then add the sauce.

Stir-fry for 1 more minute, then return the tofu to the wok. Sprinkle the sesame oil over it and cook, stirring, for 1 minute for the tofu to absorb some of the flavours from the sauce. Serve immediately.

For spiced pork & tofu stir-fry, mix the oyster sauce and fry the tofu as above. Stir-fry 125 g (4 oz) thinly sliced pork fillet in 2 tablespoons vegetable oil, then tip in 1 teaspoon hot chilli powder and the garlic, ginger and spring onions. Continue the recipe as above, omitting the water chestnuts.

tofu with chilli & tamarind

Serves **4**
Preparation time **10 minutes**
Cooking time **5 minutes**

1 tablespoon chopped **fresh
    root ginger**
1 **lemon grass stalk**, finely
    chopped
2 **garlic cloves**, chopped
2 **birds eye chillies**, chopped
1 teaspoon **dried shrimp
    paste**
2 teaspoons **tamarind paste**
1 teaspoon **salt**
1 teaspoon **caster sugar**
450 g (14½ oz) **firm tofu**
2 tablespoons **groundnut oil**
150 g (5 oz) **French beans**,
    chopped
25 g (1 oz) **toasted peanuts**,
    roughly chopped, to garnish

Blend all the ingredients up to and including the sugar in a food processor to make a paste. Tip the paste into a shallow dish.

Drain the tofu and pat it dry with kitchen paper. Cut it into 20 equal-sized cubes and gently toss it in the prepared paste. Leave to marinate for 1 hour.

Heat the oil in a wok over high heat until the oil starts to shimmer. Add the tofu and stir-fry for 2–3 minutes until golden. Add the French beans and cook for a further 30 seconds. Garnish with a scattering of peanuts before serving.

For king prawns with chilli & tamarind, replace the tofu with 250 g (8 oz) king prawns. Make the paste as above, then marinate the prawns for 1 hour before stir-frying and adding the chopped French beans as above. Omit the peanuts, garnish with coriander leaves and serve with lime wedges.

stir-fried pak choi & mushrooms

Serves **4**

Preparation time **3 minutes**

Cooking time **10 minutes**

½ tablespoon **rapeseed** or **olive oil**

500 g (1 lb) **pak choi**, halved lengthways

20 **shiitake mushrooms**, trimmed and halved

1 teaspoon **shoyu** or **tamari sauce**

1 tablespoon **Chinese rice wine** or **dry sherry**

3 tablespoons **vegetable stock**

½ tablespoon **cornflour** mixed to a paste with 1 tablespoon **water**

Heat the oil in a wok over a high heat until the oil starts to shimmer. Add the pak choi, a handful at a time, stirring occasionally. Cover the pan and cook for about 2–3 minutes, until the pak choi leaves have wilted slightly, then remove to a serving plate.

Return the wok to the heat, add the mushrooms and stir-fry over a high heat for 30 seconds. Add the shoyu sauce, rice wine and the vegetable stock and stir to mix. Add the cornflour paste slowly, stirring constantly until the sauce has thickened.

Pour the mushrooms and sauce over the pak choi and serve immediately.

For broccoli & mushrooms in a rich, spicy sauce,

replace the pak choi with 500 g (1 lb) small broccoli florets. Heat 1 tablespoon oil in a wok over a high heat, add the broccoli together with 4 tablespoons water and stir-fry for 2–3 minutes. Then stir in the mushrooms. After 30 seconds add the other ingredients, adding 2 tablespoons oyster sauce to the wok with the shoyu sauce. Stir 1 teaspoon Chinese chilli oil into the finished dish just before serving.

rice & noodles

egg fried rice

Serves **4** with 1 other dish
Preparation time **5 minutes**
Cooking time **4 minutes**

4 **eggs**
2 teaspoons chopped **fresh root ginger**
1½ tablespoons **light soy sauce**
2 tablespoons **groundnut oil**
300 g (10 oz) cold cooked **jasmine rice** (200 g/7 oz raw weight)
2 **spring onions**, finely sliced
¼ teaspoon **sesame oil**

Place the eggs, ginger and half the soy sauce in a bowl and whisk lightly to combine.

Heat the oil in a wok over a high heat until the oil starts to shimmer. Pour in the egg mixture and use a spatula to scramble it for 30–60 seconds, until just cooked.

Add the cold cooked rice, the spring onions, sesame oil and remaining soy sauce and stir-fry for 1–2 minutes, until the rice is steaming hot.

For fried rice with Chinese leaves & chilli, follow the recipe as above, adding 1 sliced red chilli and 125 g (4 oz) shredded Chinese leaves once the rice is hot, and stir-frying for a further 30 seconds.

prawn fried rice

Serves **4** with 1 other dish
Preparation time **5 minutes**
Cooking time **7 minutes**

1 tablespoon **rapeseed** or
  olive oil
500 g (1 lb) raw peeled **tiger
  prawns**
50 g (2 oz) **shiitake** or **button
  mushrooms**, trimmed and
  halved
1 **courgette**, thinly sliced
1 small **carrot**, thinly sliced
50 g (2 oz) **green beans**, cut
  into 2.5 cm (1 inch) pieces
300 g (10 oz) cold cooked
  jasmine rice (200 g/7 oz
  raw weight)
2 teaspoons **shoyu** or **tamari
  sauce**
1 teaspoon freshly ground
  black pepper
1 **spring onion**, thinly sliced,
  to garnish

Heat the oil in a wok over a high heat until the oil
starts to shimmer. Stir-fry the prawns for 1 minute,
then remove using a slotted spoon and set aside.

Add the mushrooms, courgette, carrot and green
beans and stir-fry for 2 minutes over a high heat.
Stir in the cold cooked rice and the shoyu sauce,
season with pepper and mix thoroughly.

Return the prawns to the wok and stir-fry the rice
mixture for a couple of minutes. Garnish with spring
onion slices and serve.

For warming prawn, rice & mushroom soup,

stir-fry the prawns and vegetables as described
above. When the vegetables are cooked, add 750 ml
(1 1/4 pints) vegetable stock, 1/2 teaspoon caster sugar,
2 tablespoons shoyu and 2 thick slices of fresh root
ginger to the wok. Boil for 10 minutes, then stir in the
rice, return the prawns to the pan and season with
pepper. Simmer gently until the rice is hot, then
garnish with the spring onion and serve.

chinese pork & prawn fried rice

Serves **4** with 1 other dish
Preparation time **5 minutes**
Cooking time **5 minutes**

4 **eggs**
1½ teaspoons **sesame oil**
2 teaspoons **light soy sauce**
pinch of **salt**
1 tablespoon **groundnut oil**
125 g (4 oz) raw peeled
   prawns
125 g (4 oz) **ham**, shredded
1 tablespoon chopped **fresh
   root ginger**
2 **garlic cloves**, crushed
5 **spring onions**, finely sliced
300 g (10 oz) cold cooked
   jasmine rice (200 g/7 oz
   raw weight)

Place the eggs, 1 teaspoon of the sesame oil, the soy sauce and salt in a bowl and whisk lightly to combine.

Heat ½ tablespoon of the groundnut oil in a wok over a high heat until the oil starts to shimmer. Pour in the egg mixture and use a spatula to scramble it for 30–60 seconds, until just cooked, then remove the eggs and set aside.

Return the wok to the hob and heat the remaining oil. Add the prawns, ham, ginger and garlic and stir-fry for 1 minute, until the prawns look pink. Add the spring onions, cold cooked rice, cooked eggs and remaining sesame oil and stir-fry for 1–2 minutes, until the rice is steaming hot.

For chicken fried rice, omit the prawns and ham. Cook the eggs as above and remove from the wok, then heat 1 tablespoon groundnut oil and stir-fry the ginger, garlic and 250 g (8 oz) finely chopped chicken breast for 2–3 minutes. Add 2 tablespoons oyster sauce and cook for 1 minute, then tip in the spring onions and rice and complete the recipe as above.

thai chicken & basil fried rice

Serves **4** with 1 other dish
Preparation time **5 minutes**
Cooking time **7 minutes**

150 g (5 oz) **minced chicken**
2 tablespoons **groundnut oil**
2 **garlic cloves**, chopped
2 **shallots**, thinly sliced
2 **birds eye chillies**, finely
  chopped
1 **red pepper**, cored,
  deseeded and cut into small
  cubes
2 tablespoons **Thai fish
  sauce (nam pla)**
½ teaspoon **demerara sugar**
1½ tablespoons **light soy
  sauce**
300 g (10 oz) cold cooked
  jasmine rice (200 g/7 oz
  raw weight)
large handful of **Thai basil
  leaves**

Break up the chicken mince with a fork and set aside.

Heat the oil in a wok over a high heat until the oil starts to shimmer. Add the garlic, shallots, chilli and red pepper and stir-fry for 30 seconds, then add the chicken, fish sauce, sugar and soy sauce. Stir-fry for 3–4 minutes, until the chicken is lightly golden.

Add the cold cooked rice and the basil and stir gently until the rice is steaming hot and the aroma of the basil is released.

For cubed pork fried rice with herbs, chop 200 g (7 oz) lean pork into small cubes and use instead of the chicken. Cook as above, reducing the basil by half and adding a handful of coriander leaves and 6 torn mint leaves.

vegetable fried rice with roast pork

Serves **4**
Preparation time **5 minutes**
Cooking time **8 minutes**

500 g (1 lb) boneless, skinless
  pork loin
2 tablespoons **Chinese red
  wine vinegar** or **balsamic
  vinegar**
1 tablespoon **fennel seeds**
½ tablespoon **olive oil**
1 tablespoon crushed
  Szechuan peppercorns

Vegetable fried rice
2 tablespoons **groundnut oil**
150 g (5 oz) **carrots**, diced
1 **egg**, beaten
1 recipe quantity cold **boiled
  rice** (see right)
100 g (3½ oz) **frozen peas**,
  thawed
100 g (3½ oz) canned
  sweetcorn kernels, drained
100 g (3½ oz) canned
  pineapple chunks, drained
1 tablespoon **shoyu** or **tamari
  sauce**
½ teaspoon **white pepper**
2 tablespoons chopped
  spring onions

Put the pork in a roasting tin with the vinegar, fennel seeds and olive oil. Sprinkle with the crushed peppercorns and set aside to marinate for 30 minutes.

Cook the pork in a preheated oven, 220°C (425°F), Gas Mark 7, for 40 minutes or until cooked.

Heat the oil in a wok over a medium heat. Stir-fry the carrots for 1 minute, then add the beaten egg.

Add the cold cooked rice, the peas, sweetcorn and pineapple and stir-fry for about 5 minutes. Season with shoyu or tamari sauce and white pepper, stir in the spring onions and serve with the roast pork.

For perfect boiled rice, to serve 4, put 200 g (7 oz) Thai jasmine or long-grain rice in a sieve and wash it under running warm water, rubbing the grains together between your hands to get rid of any excess starch. Put the rice in a saucepan and add water to a level of 2.5 cm (1 inch) above the rice. Place the pan on the smallest ring on the hob and bring it to the boil. Give it a quick stir, then reduce the heat to a simmer. Cover with a lid and leave to cook for 10 minutes. Turn off the heat and allow the rice to steam with the lid on for another 10 minutes. Don't be tempted to lift the lid to check what's going on. To serve, fluff up the grains of rice with a spoon or fork.

prawn nasi goreng

Serves **4**

Preparation time **10 minutes**

Cooking time **13 minutes**

5 tablespoons **groundnut oil**

2 **eggs**, beaten

4 **shallots**, sliced

1 **red chilli**, deseeded and cut into thin strips

1 tablespoon chopped **fresh root ginger**

1 teaspoon **ground coriander**

1 teaspoon **paprika**

1 **carrot**, finely diced

300 g (10 oz) **white cabbage**, thinly sliced

1 tablespoon **light soy sauce**

1 tablespoon **tomato ketchup**

300 g (10 oz) cold cooked **jasmine rice** (200 g/7 oz raw weight)

200 g (7 oz) peeled cooked **prawns**

1 tablespoon snipped **chives**

Heat 1 tablespoon of the oil in a wok over a moderate heat. Add the egg mixture and swirl so it spreads thinly over the surface of the pan. Let it set for about 30 seconds, then loosen the edges with a fish slice and flip over. Cook for 10 seconds, remove to a chopping board, roll up and slice into ribbons. Set aside.

Heat the wok over a medium heat, add the remaining oil and, once it begins to shimmer, stir-fry the shallots for 4–5 minutes until golden and crisp. Remove with a slotted spoon and drain on kitchen paper. Set aside.

Drain all but 1 tablespoon of the oil from the pan. Toss in the chilli, ginger, ground coriander and paprika and stir-fry for 30 seconds. Add the carrot and cabbage and stir-fry for 2 minutes, then add the soy sauce and ketchup. Cook for 1 more minute, then toss in the cold cooked rice, the prawns and half the snipped chives. Cook for a further 2 minutes, until the rice is steaming hot. Serve with the fried shallots, egg strips and reserved chives scattered over the top.

For chicken nasi goreng with cucumber, omit the prawns and follow the first 2 steps of the recipe as above. Cut 300 g (10 oz) boneless, skinless chicken breasts into small cubes and fry with the chilli, fresh ginger and spices before completing the recipe. Cut a 5 cm (2 inch) piece cucumber into quarters lengthways then slice thinly. Toss into the rice just before garnishing as above.

beef & vegetable fried rice

Serves **4**
Preparation time **10 minutes**
Cooking time **8 minutes**

2 tablespoons **groundnut oil**
2 **garlic cloves**, crushed
2 **birds eye chillies**, finely
  chopped
2 **shallots**, cut into thin
  wedges
250 g (8 oz) lean **beef**, cut
  into thin strips
1 **green pepper**, cored,
  deseeded and cut into strips
125 g (4 oz) **baby sweetcorn**,
  cut in half lengthways
125 g (4 oz) **straw
  mushrooms**, trimmed
2 tablespoons **Thai fish
  sauce (nam pla)**
½ teaspoon **demerara sugar**
1 tablespoon **light soy sauce**
300 g (10 oz) cold cooked
  jasmine rice (200 g/7 oz
  raw weight)
4 **spring onions** cut into thin
  rounds
handful of **coriander leaves**,
  torn

Heat the oil in a wok over a high heat until the oil starts to shimmer. Add the garlic, chillies, shallots and beef and cook for 2–3 minutes, until the beef begins to colour. Tip in the pepper, sweetcorn and mushrooms and cook for a further 2 minutes.

Stir in the fish sauce, sugar and soy sauce and cook for a few more seconds, then add the cold cooked rice and the spring onions, stir-frying until the rice is steaming hot. Fold in the coriander and serve.

For oriental vegetable fried rice, omit the beef. Cook the garlic, chilli and shallots for a few seconds, then stir in the vegetables, adding 125 g (4 oz) sliced broccoli florets and 75 g (3 oz) bean sprouts. Complete the recipe as above.

spicy mixed noodles

Serves **4**
Preparation time **10 minutes**
Cooking time **10 minutes**

250 g (8 oz) **thin dried rice
    noodles**
2 teaspoons **sesame oil**
2 tablespoons **groundnut oil**
3 **garlic cloves**, crushed
1 tablespoon chopped **fresh
    root ginger**
1 **red onion**, finely sliced
1 **red chilli**, cut into thin strips
75 g (3 oz) **shiitake
    mushrooms**, finely diced
150 g (5 oz) **ham**
150 g (5 oz) peeled cooked
    prawns
75 g (3 oz) **fresh** or **frozen
    peas**, defrosted if frozen
200 g (7 oz) **bean sprouts**
4 **spring onions**, finely sliced
handful of **coriander leaves**,
    roughly chopped

Spicy sauce
1½ tablespoons **Madras curry
    paste**
2 tablespoons **light soy sauce**
2 tablespoons **Chinese rice
    wine** or **dry sherry**
½ teaspoon **salt**

Combine all the spicy sauce ingredients and set aside.

Cook the noodles in a large pan of boiling water, according to the packet instructions. Refresh in cold running water, then drain and toss into a bowl with the sesame oil.

Heat the groundnut oil in a wok over a high heat until the oil starts to shimmer. Add the garlic, ginger, onion and chilli and give the ingredients a good stir. Tip in the mushrooms and stir-fry for 1 minute, then add the ham, prawns, peas and bean sprouts. Stir for 1 minute.

Pour in the prepared sauce and toss well to combine, then stir in the cooked noodles, spring onions and coriander. Stir until the noodles are heated through, then serve.

For luxury spicy mixed noodles, replace the small prawns with 200 g (7 oz) raw peeled king prawns and 150 g (5 oz) quartered scallops, and leave the shiitake mushrooms whole. Cook as above, adding the prawns and scallops with the mushrooms and cooking for a further 2 minutes before adding the remaining ingredients.

thai stir-fried noodles

Serves **4**
Preparation time **12 minutes**
Cooking time **12 minutes**

125 g (4 oz) **thin dried rice
  noodles**
2 tablespoons **rapeseed** or
  olive oil
2 **garlic cloves**, crushed
1 tablespoon chopped **fresh
  root ginger**
1 heaped tablespoon **medium
  curry paste**
250 g (8 oz) **baby sweetcorn**
250 g (8 oz) **pointed
  cabbage**, finely sliced
1 small **red pepper**, cored,
  deseeded and finely sliced
1½ teaspoons **Thai fish sauce
  (nam pla)**
2 teaspoons **shoyu** or **tamari
  sauce**
60 ml (2½ fl oz) canned **light
  coconut milk**
100 g (3½ oz) **roasted,
  unsalted peanuts**, chopped
2 tablespoons chopped
  coriander leaves, plus
  sprigs to garnish
4 **spring onions**, finely sliced
2 tablespoons **lime juice**

Put the rice noodles into a bowl of boiling water, cover
and leave to stand for 5 minutes for them to soften.
Drain and set aside.

Heat the oil in a wok over a high heat until the oil
starts to shimmer. Add the garlic, ginger and curry
paste and stir-fry for 2–3 minutes until the spices
become fragrant.

Add the sweetcorn, cabbage and red pepper and
stir-fry for about 5 minutes or until the cabbage
has started to soften and wilt.

Add the fish sauce, shoyu sauce and coconut milk. Stir
to mix, then toss in the rice noodles and stir-fry until
they have warmed through. Turn off the heat and gently
stir in the peanuts, coriander, spring onions and lime
juice. Garnish with coriander sprigs.

For zesty noodles with hot smoked salmon, follow
the recipe above but add the grated rind of 2 limes to
the water when soaking the noodles and add 200 g
(7 oz) flaked hot smoked salmon to the wok together
with the cooked noodles.

rice noodles with aromatic prawns

Serves **4**

Preparation time **10 minutes**

Cooking time **7 minutes**

400 g (13 oz) raw peeled
  tiger prawns

2 tablespoons **olive oil**

400 g (13 oz) **thin dried rice
  noodles**

4 **garlic cloves**, chopped

3 **red chillies**, chopped

2 **lemon grass stalks**, chopped

2 **onions**, shredded

6 **celery stalks**, shredded

4 teaspoons **shoyu sauce**

3 **spring onions**, shredded

black pepper

Lemon & fish sauce

2 **red chillies**, chopped

½ **garlic clove**, crushed

60 ml (2 fl oz) **lemon juice**

60 ml (2 fl oz) **Thai fish sauce**

3 tablespoons **light
  muscovado sugar**

125 ml (4 fl oz) **water**

To garnish

4 tablespoons crushed
  roasted unsalted peanuts

2 **red chillies**, split

Mix the prawns with 1 tablespoon of the olive oil a small bowl and set aside.

Soak the rice noodles in hot water to cover and leave for about 5–10 minutes until soft. Drain well, transfer to a serving plate and keep warm.

Make the lemon and fish sauce by mixing all the sauce ingredients in a bowl. (Any sauce not used in the recipe can be kept in an airtight jar in the refrigerator for a week.)

Heat a wok until very hot, add the oil-coated prawns and sear on each side for about 30 seconds until golden brown. Remove the prawns using a slotted spoon and set aside.

Heat the remaining oil, swirling it around to coat the wok. Add the garlic, chillies and lemon grass and stir-fry for about 30 seconds until the garlic is lightly browned. Toss in the onions and celery and stir-fry for a couple of minutes, until they have softened a little.

Return the prawns to the wok, add the shoyu sauce and spring onions and season with pepper. Arrange on top of the noodles and drizzle with 3 tablespoons of the lemon and fish sauce. Garnish with the crushed peanuts and the red chillies and serve with the remaining sauce in a jug.

tofu pad thai

Serves **4**
Preparation time **15 minutes**
Cooking time **10 minutes**

200 g (7 oz) **thick dried
rice noodles**
450 g (14½ oz) **firm tofu**
vegetable oil, for deep-frying
2 **garlic cloves**, finely
chopped
3 **eggs**
juice of 1 **lime**
2 tablespoons **Thai fish
sauce (nam pla)**
½ teaspoon **demerara sugar**
50 g (2 oz) **roasted peanuts**,
crushed
2 tablespoons **dried shrimp**,
ground
75 g (3 oz) **bean sprouts**
4 **spring onions**, diagonally
sliced
1 **red chilli**, cut into thin rings
large handful of **coriander
leaves**

Soak the noodles following the packet instructions,
then drain.

Drain the tofu and pat it dry with kitchen paper, then
cut it into 20 equal-sized cubes and set aside. Pour
enough oil into a wok to deep-fry the tofu, and heat
it to 190°C (375°F), or until a cube of bread dropped
into the oil turns golden in 20 seconds. Add half the
tofu and deep-fry until puffy and golden, then remove
using a slotted spoon and drain on kitchen paper. Fry
the remaining tofu in the same way. Set aside.

Pour off all but 2 tablespoons of the oil and place
the wok over a high heat. Add the garlic and eggs and
stir-fry for a couple of seconds, then add the drained
noodles, lime juice, fish sauce, sugar, half the peanuts
and half the dried shrimp. Stir-fry for 2 minutes, until
the noodles are steaming hot, then stir in the bean
sprouts, spring onions, chilli and cooked tofu. Cook
for 1 more minute, then top with the remaining
peanuts, the dried shrimp and the coriander.

For chicken pad thai, omit the tofu and instead cut
450 g (14½ oz) boneless, skinless chicken breast
into strips. Heat 2 tablespoons groundnut oil in a wok
and use to fry the chicken strips for 2–3 minutes until
browned. Remove the chicken using a slotted spoon,
then cook the recipe as above, adding the browned
chicken with the noodles.

chicken & pak choi noodles

Serves **4**

Preparation time **10 minutes**,
plus marinating

Cooking time **7 minutes**

500 g (1 lb) boneless, skinless
chicken breasts, cut into
thin strips

1 tablespoon **Chinese rice
wine** or **dry sherry**

2 teaspoons **cornflour**

½ teaspoon **sesame oil**

½ teaspoon **salt**

2 tablespoons **groundnut oil**

5 **spring onions**, cut into
5 cm (1 inch) lengths

2.5 cm (1 inch) piece **fresh
root ginger**, cut into
matchsticks

1 **red chilli**, deseeded and
thinly sliced

1 tablespoon **sesame seeds**

3 heads of **pak choi**, cut into
5 cm (2 inch) pieces

2 tablespoons **oyster sauce**

1 tablespoon **water**

300 g (10 oz) **straight to wok
noodles**

Put the chicken in a bowl with the rice wine,
cornflour, sesame oil and salt and leave to marinate
for 30 minutes.

Heat the oil in a wok over a high heat until the oil
starts to shimmer. Tip in the chicken strips, spring
onions, ginger, chilli and sesame seeds and stir-fry for
2 minutes before adding the pak choi. Stir for 1 minute,
then add the oyster sauce and measurement water.
Cook, stirring, for 1 minute, then toss in the noodles
and stir-fry until steaming hot.

For pork & prawn noodles, replace the chicken with
325 g (11 oz) lean pork strips and marinate as above.
Follow the recipe, adding 150 g (5 oz) cooked small
prawns to the pan with the pak choi.

duck & vegetable noodles

Serves **4**

Preparation time **10 minutes**

Cooking time **15 minutes**

250 g (8 oz) **medium egg noodles**

1 teaspoon **sesame oil**

3 tablespoons **groundnut oil**

500g (1 lb) skinned **duck breasts**, cut into thin strips

1 **leek**, thinly sliced

2 **garlic cloves**, finely chopped

1 **red chilli**, cut into rings

1 tablespoon finely chopped **fresh root ginger**

200 g (7 oz) **mangetout**, halved

125 g (4 oz) **bean sprouts**

2 tablespoons **light soy sauce**

2 tablespoons **Chinese rice wine** or **dry sherry**

1 teaspoon **clear honey**

handful of **coriander leaves**, roughly chopped, plus extra whole leaves to garnish

Cook the noodles in a large pan of boiling water, according to the packet instructions. Refresh in cold running water, then drain and toss into a bowl with the sesame oil.

Heat half the groundnut oil in a wok over a high heat until the oil starts to shimmer. Add the duck breast, season with salt and stir-fry for 2–3 minutes until browned. Tip the meat on to a plate and set aside while you return the wok to the heat.

Wipe the wok clean with kitchen paper, then add the remaining oil. Once it's hot, add the leek and stir-fry for 1 minute. Toss in the garlic, ginger, chilli, mangetout and bean sprouts and stir-fry for 1 minute. Return the meat to the pan, pour in the soy sauce, rice wine and honey and stir-fry for 1 minute. Finally, add the noodles and chopped coriander, stirring until the noodles are steaming hot. Garnish with a few whole coriander leaves and serve.

For duck with rice noodles & coconut milk, replace the egg noodles with 200 g (7 oz) thick dried rice noodles, soaked following packet instructions. Replace the soy sauce and rice wine with 5 tablespoons coconut milk and 1 tablespoon fish sauce. Simmer for 3 minutes before adding the noodles.

chicken & vegetable fried noodles

Serves **2**
Preparation time **10 minutes**
Cooking time **15 minutes**

- 1 tablespoon **cornflour**
- 1 tablespoon **Thai fish sauce (nam pla)**
- 1 tablespoon **dark soy sauce**
- 1 teaspoon **demerara sugar**
- 100 ml (3½ fl oz) **vegetable stock**
- 150 g (5 oz) **thin egg noodles**
- **vegetable oil**, for deep-frying
- 2 **garlic cloves**, finely chopped
- 175 g (6 oz) boneless, skinless **chicken thighs**, cut into thin strips
- 75 g (3 oz) **straw mushrooms**, trimmed
- 75 g (3 oz) **baby sweetcorn**, cut in half lengthways
- 75 g (3 oz) 1 **red pepper**, cored, deseeded and cut into small cubes
- 4 **spring onions**, cut into 2.5 cm (1 inch) lengths
- **coriander sprigs**, to garnish

Combine the cornflour, fish sauce and soy sauce to make a paste. Stir in the sugar and stock and set aside.

Cook the noodles in a large pan of boiling water, according to the packet instructions. Refresh in cold running water, then drain thoroughly.

Pour enough oil into a wok to deep-fry the noodles, and heat it to 190°C (375°F), or until a cube of bread dropped into the oil turns golden in 20 seconds. Add half the noodles and deep-fry they are until crisp and golden, then remove using a slotted spoon and drain on kitchen paper. Stir-fry the remaining noodles in the same way. Place on a warm serving dish.

Pour off all but 2 tablespoons of the oil and place the wok over a high heat. Add the garlic and chicken and stir-fry for 2 minutes, then tip in the remaining ingredients, except for the coriander. Stir-fry for a further 2 minutes, then pour in the prepared sauce and bring to the boil. As soon as the sauce starts to thicken, spoon the stir-fry over the crispy noodles and garnish with coriander sprigs.

For Thai chicken noodle salad, make a dressing by mixing the fish sauce, soy sauce, sugar, ½ teaspoon sesame oil, 2 tablespoons light olive oil and the juice of 1 lime. Stir into the refreshed noodles, adding all the raw vegetables, garlic and spring onions. Stir-fry the chicken in 1 tablespoon groundnut oil for 3–4 minutes until cooked through and toss into the salad.

singapore noodles

Serves **4**
Preparation time **10 minutes**
Cooking time **10 minutes**

5 tablespoons **vegetable oil**
2 **eggs**, beaten
6 **shallots**, thinly sliced
1 **onion**, chopped
3 **garlic cloves**, crushed
2 tablespoons **black bean sauce**
2 tablespoons **Chinese rice wine** or **dry sherry**
1 **red chilli**, finely chopped
½ teaspoon **Chinese five-spice powder**
600 ml (1 pint) **stock** or **water**
250 g (8 oz) **fresh egg noodles**
150 g (5 oz) **bean sprouts**
250 g (8 oz) **char siu pork** or **barbecue pork**, sliced
125 g (4 oz) **pak choi**, chopped
125 g (4 oz) raw peeled **tiger prawns**
½ teaspoon **salt**
2 **red chillies**, sliced
coriander leaves
sweet chilli sauce, to serve

Heat 1 tablespoon of the oil in a wok over a moderate heat. Add the egg mixture and swirl so it spreads thinly over the surface of the pan. Let it set for about 30 seconds, then loosen the edges with a fish slice and flip over. Cook for 10 seconds, remove to a chopping board, roll up and slice into ribbons. Set aside.

Add 4 tablespoons oil and, once it begins to shimmer, stir-fry the shallots for 4–5 minutes until golden and crisp. Remove with a slotted spoon and drain on kitchen paper. Set aside.

Drain all but 1 tablespoon of the oil from the pan. Add the onion and stir-fry until beginning to brown. Add the garlic, black bean sauce, rice wine, chilli and Chinese five-spice powder and stir-fry for 2 minutes.

Add the stock, noodles and bean sprouts and bring to the boil, tossing the noodles and bean sprouts in the stock.

Add the pork to the wok with the green vegetables, prawns and salt and cook for a further 4 minutes. Top with the deep-fried shallots, shredded omelette, sliced chillies and coriander leaves and serve with sweet chilli sauce.

For special fried rice, replace the noodles with 250 g (8 oz) cooked jasmine rice. Cook as above, omitting the stock and only adding the rice to the wok once the prawns have cooked for 3 minutes. Stir-fry until steaming hot.

crispy noodles with beef

Serves **4**

Preparation time **10 minutes**,
   plus marinating

Cooking time **20 minutes**

½ teaspoon **clear honey**, such
   as acacia

2 tablespoons **light soy
   sauce**

2 tablespoons **oyster sauce**

2 tablespoons **Chinese rice
   wine** or **dry sherry**

2 teaspoons **cornflour**

400 g (14 oz) lean **beef**,
   trimmed and cut into strips

250 g (8 oz) **medium egg
   noodles**

1 teaspoon **toasted sesame
   oil**

4 tablespoons **groundnut oil**

2 teaspoons **fresh root
   ginger**, chopped

2 **garlic cloves**, chopped

1 **leek**, thinly sliced

200 g (7 oz) **broccoli florets**,
   sliced

3 tablespoons **water**

Mix together the honey, soy sauce, oyster sauce, rice wine and cornflour. Pour half the sauce into a bowl, add the beef and stir well. Cover and marinate in the refrigerator for 30 minutes.

Cook the noodles in boiling water, according to the packet instructions. Refresh in cold running water and drain well, then moisten with the sesame oil. Set aside.

Heat 2 tablespoons oil in a wok over a high heat until the oil starts to shimmer. Add the noodles and cook for about 5 minutes, until the underside is golden. Flip the 'cake' over and cook for about 3 minutes, until pale gold. Place on a warm serving plate.

Heat another tablespoon of the oil as before and add the beef. Stir-fry for about 2 minutes, then tip out on to a plate along with any juices.

Wash the wok quickly and reheat on the hob until dry. Heat the remaining oil and add the ginger, garlic and leek. Stir-fry for 1 minute, then add the broccoli and stir-fry for 2 minutes. Pour in the reserved sauce mixture and measurement water and bring to the boil. Return the beef to the wok and stir for 1 minute. Tip the mixture over the noodles and serve immediately.

For crispy noodles with glazed vegetables, omit
the beef. Make the sauce and cook the noodles as above. Heat 1 tablespoon oil and stir-fry the ginger, garlic and leek for 1 minute before adding the broccoli, 1 red and 1 green pepper, cubed, and 200 g (7 oz) sliced courgette. Stir-fry for 2 minutes. Add the reserved sauce mixture and measurement water and stir for 1 minute before serving over the noodles.

index

acknowledgements

Executive editor: Nicky Hill
Senior editor: Fiona Robertson
Deputy art director: Karen Sawyer
Designer: Rebecca Johns, Cobalt id
Photographer: Will Heap
Food stylist: Marina Filippelli
Props stylist: Liz Hippisley
Senior production controller: Manjit Sihra

Special photography: © Octopus Publishing Group
Limited/Will Heap

Other photography: Octopus Publishing Group
Limited/David Loftus 89, 233; /Peter Myers 27, 51, 53,
81, 101, 109, 113, 149; 155, 161; /William Reavell 25,
39, 79, 85, 117, 134, 141, 145, 173, 177, 195, 201,
207, 211, 221, 223; /Ian Wallace 127, 131, 165.